Y0-DTB-552

ADULT BIBLE TEACHING GUIDE

The Gospel of Matthew
HOPE IN THE RESURRECTED CHRIST

EBBIE SMITH
VERNON DAVIS
EMILY MARTIN
BOBBY BRAGG
RONNY MARRIOTT

BAPTISTWAYPRESS®

Dallas, Texas

The Gospel of Matthew: Hope in the Resurrected Christ—Adult Bible Teaching Guide

BAPTISTWAY PRESS˙ Management Team
Executive Director, Baptist General Convention of Texas: Randel Everett
Director, Missions, Evangelism, and Ministry Team: Wayne Shuffield
Ministry Team Leader: Phil Miller
Publisher, BAPTISTWAY PRESS˙: Ross West

Cover and Interior Design and Production: Desktop Miracles, Inc.
Printing: Data Reproductions Corporation

First edition: December 2008
ISBN–13: 978–1–934731–22–2

How to Make the Best Use of This Teaching Guide

Leading a class in studying the Bible is a sacred trust. This *Teaching Guide* has been prepared to help you as you give your best to this important task.

In each lesson, you will find first "Bible Comments" for teachers, to aid you in your study and preparation. The three sections of "Bible Comments" are "Understanding the Context," "Interpreting the Scriptures," and "Focusing on the Meaning." "Understanding the Context" provides a summary overview of the entire background passage that also sets the passage in the context of the Bible book being studied. "Interpreting the Scriptures" provides verse-by-verse comments on the focal passage. "Focusing on the Meaning" offers help with the meaning and application of the focal text.

The second main part of each lesson is "Teaching Plans." You'll find two complete teaching plans in this section. The first is called "Teaching Plan—Varied Learning Activities," and the second is called "Teaching Plan—Lecture and Questions." Choose the plan that best fits your class and your style of teaching. You may also use and adapt ideas from both. Each plan is intended to be practical, helpful, and immediately useful as you prepare to teach.

The major headings in each teaching plan are intended to help you sequence how you teach so as to follow the flow of how people tend to learn. The first major heading, "Connect with Life," provides ideas that will help you begin the class session where your class is and draw your class into the study. The second major heading, "Guide Bible Study," offers suggestions for helping your class engage the Scriptures actively and develop a greater understanding of this portion of the Bible's message. The third major heading, "Encourage Application," is meant to help participants focus on how to respond with their lives to this message.

As you begin the study with your class, be sure to find a way to help your class know the date on which each lesson will be studied. You might use one or more of the following methods:

- In the first session of the study, briefly overview the study by identifying with your class the date on which each lesson will be studied. Lead your class to write the date in the table of contents in their *Study Guides* and on the first page of each lesson.
- Make and post a chart that indicates the date on which each lesson will be studied.
- If all of your class has e-mail, send them an e-mail with the dates the lessons will be studied.
- Provide a bookmark with the lesson dates. You may want to include information about your church and then use the bookmark as an outreach tool, too. A model for a bookmark can be downloaded from www.baptistwaypress.org on the Resources for Adults page.
- Develop a sticker with the lesson dates, and place it on the table of contents or on the back cover.

Here are some steps you can take to help you prepare well to teach each lesson and save time in doing so:

1. Start early in the week before your class meets.

2. If your church's adult Bible study teachers meet for lesson overview and preparation, plan to participate. If your church's adult Bible study teachers don't have this planning time now, look for ways to begin. You, your fellow teachers, and your church will benefit from this mutual encouragement and preparation.

3. Overview the study in the *Study Guide*. Look at the table of contents, and see where this lesson fits in the overall study. Then read or review the study introduction to the book that is being studied.

4. Consider carefully the suggested Main Idea, Question to Explore, and Teaching Aim. These can help you discover the main thrust of this particular lesson.

5. Use your Bible to read and consider prayerfully the Scripture passages for the lesson. Using your Bible in your study and in the class session can provide a positive model to class members to use their own Bibles and give more attention to Bible study themselves. (Each writer of the Bible comments in both the *Teaching Guide* and the *Study Guide* has chosen a favorite translation. You're free to use the Bible translation you prefer and compare it with the translations chosen, of course.)

6. After reading all the Scripture passages in your Bible, then read the Bible comments in the *Study Guide*. The Bible comments are intended to be an aid to your study of the Bible. Read also the small articles—"sidebars"—in each lesson. They are intended to provide additional, enrichment information and inspiration and to encourage thought and application. Try to answer for yourself the questions included in each lesson. They're intended to encourage further thought and application, and you can also use them in the class session itself. Continue your Bible study with the aid of the Bible comments included in this *Teaching Guide*.

7. Review the "Teaching Plans" in this *Teaching Guide*. Consider how these suggestions would help you teach this Bible passage in your class to accomplish the teaching aim.

8. Consider prayerfully the needs of your class, and think about how to teach so you can help your class learn best.

9. Develop and follow a lesson plan based on the suggestions in this *Teaching Guide*, with alterations as needed for your class.

10. Enjoy leading your class in discovering the meaning of the Scripture passages and in applying these passages to their lives.

FREE! Additional adult Bible study comments by Dr. Jim Denison, pastor of Park Cities Baptist Church, Dallas, Texas, are online at www.baptistwaypress.org and can be downloaded free. These lessons are posted on the internet a week in advance of the first Sunday of use.

FREE! Downloadable teaching resource items for use in your class are available at www.baptistwaypress.org! Watch for them in "Teaching

Plans" for each lesson. Then go online to www.baptistwaypress.org and click on "Teaching Resource Items" for this study. These items are selected from "Teaching Plans." They are provided online to make lesson preparation easier for hand-outs and similar items. Permission is granted to download these teaching resource items, print them out, copy them as needed, and use them in your class.

ALSO FREE! An additional teaching plan by Dennis Parrott, longtime Christian education leader, is available each week at www.baptistwaypress.org.

IN ADDITION: Enrichment teaching help is provided in the internet edition of the *Baptist Standard*. Access the ***FREE*** internet information by checking the *Baptist Standard* website at www.baptiststandard.com. Call 214–630–4571 to begin your subscription to the printed edition of the *Baptist Standard*.

Writers of This Teaching Guide

Ebbie Smith, writer of "Bible Comments" for lessons one through five and the bonus lesson, is retired as professor of Christian Ethics and Missions, Southwestern Baptist Theological Seminary. Dr. Smith also served fifteen years as a missionary in Indonesia. He is a veteran writer of Bible study curriculum materials for BAPTISTWAY PRESS®.

Vernon Davis wrote "Bible Comments" for lessons six through twelve. A veteran curriculum writer, he is retired as dean of the Logsdon School of Theology, Hardin-Simmons University, Abilene, Texas. Dr. Davis has also served as pastor of First Baptist Church, Alexandria, Virginia, and as professor and dean at Midwestern Baptist Theological Seminary, Kansas City, Missouri.

Emily Martin wrote "Teaching Plans" for lessons one through five. She is a professional writer specializing in business and Christian communication, and she has written several assignments for BAPTISTWAY PRESS® She holds both B.A. and M.B.A. degrees from Southern Methodist University and a Th.M. from Dallas Theological Seminary. She and her husband have a son and a daughter and are members of Park Cities Baptist Church, Dallas, Texas.

Bobby Bragg, the writer of "Teaching Plans" for lessons six through nine, is associate pastor of discipleship, Broadmoor Baptist Church, Madison, Mississippi. He has served other churches in Kentucky, Georgia, and Tennessee. He has written several sets of teaching plans for BAPTISTWAY PRESS®.

Ronny Marriott, the writer of "Teaching Plans" for lessons ten through twelve and the bonus lesson, is the senior pastor of Shady Oaks Baptist Church, Hurst, Texas. He holds the Doctor of Ministry degree from Southwestern Baptist Theological Seminary. He and his wife Robin have three children. Dr. Marriott has written youth Bible study materials for BAPTISTWAY PRESS®.

The Gospel of Matthew: Hope in the Resurrected Christ

UNIT FOUR

Hope in Jesus' Glorification

FOCAL TEXT
Matthew 1:1–6, 16–17

BACKGROUND
Matthew 1:1–17

MAIN IDEA
Jesus fulfills the Messianic hope of historic Judaism and is for all people everywhere.

QUESTION TO EXPLORE
How can we say Jesus is the Messiah for all people everywhere?

TEACHING AIM
To lead the class to explain what Jesus' genealogy means and to decide on at least one way they will participate in Jesus' mission to all people

LESSON ONE
The Messiah for All People

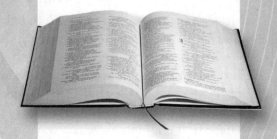

UNIT ONE
Hope in Jesus' Birth

BIBLE COMMENTS

Understanding the Context

"The Gospel According to Matthew" was written by a Jewish Christian with an extensive knowledge of and strong interest in the Old Testament. The intended audience was Jewish Christians who needed to be reminded of the close ties between the Christian faith and the Old Testament promises that Jesus came to fulfill. The Apostle Matthew is the most likely author of the book.

The central idea and key to Matthew's Gospel was that in Jesus, God's eternal purposes had come to fulfillment. The Old Testament points forward to him. He fulfills the law. Through Jesus, God will realize his plans. All history must be seen as the working out of Jesus' ministry. The fulfillment of God's purposes and gracious acts comes only through Jesus. Jesus brought a new age, and nothing was the same after his coming.

Matthew often quoted and alluded to the Old Testament. Ten times he used *formula-quotations* that stated, "then was fulfilled" or "this was to fulfill" connected with the name of a prophet or to a psalm (see Matthew 1:22–23; 2:15, 17–18, 23; 4:14–16; 8:17; 12:17–21; 21:4–5; 27:9–10).[1]

Matthew wrote his Gospel in three basic sections: an introduction to Jesus and his ministry (Matt. 1:1—4:16); the development of his ministry (4:17—16:29); and the climax of his ministry (16:21—28:20). Although written by a Jewish Christian and containing extensive Old Testament materials, this account underlines that Jesus is not only the Christ, the Messiah for the nation of Israel, but also the Messiah for all humankind. God's love and intention for all humanity sound clearly in these pages.

Matthew explained Jesus' origins to show that Jesus fulfilled Old Testament promises and that he also is the only hope for all people. The early passages stress that Jesus is the Messiah to whom the entire Old Testament points and the Son of God for whom the entire world waits. These first chapters pave the way for the assuring statements of Jesus as the promised One of God.

Interpreting the Scriptures

Jesus Christ, Son of David, Son of Abraham, the Messiah for Israel (1:1)

The opening verse in the Gospel introduces Jesus as the primary character and describes his identity in Jewish terms. This "record of the genealogy" presents an account of the origin of Jesus.

Jewish people placed great stress on genealogies, a person's lineage, and family histories. The Old Testament often contains such listings of family relationships (see Genesis 4:17–24; 5:3–32). Josephus, the first-century A.D. Jewish historian, stated his ancestry in his autobiography. Priests had to show pure lineage. The Jewish people would place much store on the fact that Jesus' lineage was directly attached to Abraham and David.

Matthew used three key titles to describe Jesus in this first verse. The opening title, "Christ," the translation of the Hebrew *Messiah*, means *the Anointed One*. The term "Christ" expressed the truth that God would appoint One through whom he would fulfill his promises and provide salvation for his people. While most Jews in the days of Jesus' earthly life were expecting a warrior-king who would free Israel from domination, Jesus came as the righteous Messiah who would free all humankind from sin. In the first fourteen verses of this gospel, Matthew provided scriptural evidence that linked Jesus to Abraham and David, from whom the Messiah was predicted to come.

The designation of Jesus as "son of David" points both to the royal role and to the necessary lineage of the Messiah. The New Testament stresses the importance of Jesus as the son of David (Acts 2:29–36; Romans 1:3; 2 Timothy 2:8; Revelation 22:16). The common people often referred to Jesus as son of David, showing they were accepting him as God's Messiah.

The words "son of Abraham" trace Jesus' ancestry back to the father of the people of Israel. This designation relates to the promise to Abraham that his offspring would be extensive. Even more, through his offspring all the peoples of the earth would be blessed. "Son of Abraham" also carried messianic overtones.

In this beginning verse, Matthew presented in a nutshell all the themes from chapters 1 and 2. The titles present Jesus as the fulfillment of the hopes and prophecies to Israel. These titles also related directly to God's mission to the entire world, including non-Jewish peoples.

Jesus Christ, the Messiah for All Peoples (1:2–6)

The genealogy that began with verse 1 validates the claims that Jesus is the son of Abraham and the son of David. King David is central in this genealogy. Adding the numerical equivalents to the consonants in David's Hebrew name, transliterated *DVD*, one comes up with 4 plus 6 plus 4 for a total numerical value of 14. The use of letters as a code for numbers was common among the Jews.

Using the theme of fourteen continues in the genealogy. Verse 17 speaks of three sets of fourteen generations. David is the fourteenth name mentioned in the first set. The symbolical emphasis points to the perfection and completion of God's dealing with world history and especially the people of Israel.

The genealogy in Matthew basically follows 1 Chronicles 1:34; 2:1–15; 3:10–17; and Ezra 3:2. Matthew's genealogy differs from that found in some Old Testament narratives and that found in Luke's Gospel. Matthew obviously omitted several names. These differences stem from neither error nor deception. The use of historical facts to emphasize religious truth was a common and accepted procedure among the Jews. Matthew was presenting the names of the people in Jesus' lineage to achieve literary symmetry. The phrase "was the father of" could mean *was an ancestor of.* Matthew shows the pattern that Jesus was the legitimate successor to the throne of David.

A notable factor in Matthew's genealogy relates to the unusual and unnecessary inclusion of five women into the lineage. Four of these are from the Old Testament. Mary the mother of Jesus is the fifth. Although some Old Testament presentations of genealogies also contain women, the presence of the names of these women in the ancestry is a surprising and extraordinary phenomenon. Most likely, none of these four women from the Old Testament were Jewish. Tamar was likely a Canaanite (see Gen. 38; 1 Chron. 2:4). She deceived her father-in-law into producing the twins, Perez and Zerah. Perez became an ancestor of Christ (Matt. 1:2–3).

Salmon was the father of Boaz. The mother of Boaz was Rahab. Although not without difficulties, some believe that this Rahab was likely the harlot of Jericho (Joshua 2:1–7). Boaz was the father of Obed, whose mother was Ruth (Matt. 1:6). Ruth was a Moabite (Ruth 1:4). David was the father of Solomon, whose mother was Bathsheba. Bathsheba had been Uriah's wife (2 Samuel 11). David took her from Uriah by cruel and inhuman tactics. Bathsheba was probably, like her husband, a Hittite.

Several reasons might have led Matthew to mention these particular women. First, he may have been emphasizing that the message of Jesus Christ would reach both Jewish and Gentile people. Here, in the very ancestry of the Savior, one finds non-Jewish women. A second reason might be that some of these women were guilty of sinful actions. Matthew showed that God can use for his purposes and his plan even people who have sinned grievously. Matthew may well have been indicating that in Jesus Christ, God had set in motion the gospel of salvation that would witness the breaking down of the barrier between Jew and Gentile and between male and female. Matthew denied the early rumor that Jesus was illegitimate but showed that some in the lineage of Jesus had suffered from similar suspicions.

The Birth of Jesus, Messiah for All Peoples (1:16–17)

1:16. Matthew moved from the genealogy of Jesus to the actual birth of the Savior who would be the Messiah, not just for the Jewish people but also for all humankind.

Verse 16 declares that Jacob was the father of Joseph, who was the husband of Mary. Joseph did not beget Jesus. He is listed as the husband of Mary. The text clearly announces that Jesus was born to Mary. In the next section of the book, Matthew will further attest the truth of the virgin birth of Jesus.

1:17. Verse 17 demonstrates Matthew's tendency to arrange his material in groups—usually of three or seven items. This genealogy is summarized in three groups of fourteen people each. Fourteen is twice seven. The numbers in this list do not agree perfectly with other lineages because Matthew was seeking to communicate a theological meaning rather than a statistical fact.

Matthew's arrangement of the genealogy highlights essential turning points in Israel's history: the founding of the Davidic kingdom; the loss of that kingdom in the Babylonian Captivity; and the final goal of Hebrew history in the coming of Jesus. The symmetry of the story indicates that the period of preparation was complete and the final goal had been reached. Significantly, Matthew completes his lineage statement that the ancestors from the Captivity came to fulfillment in Christ, the Messiah.

Focusing on the Meaning

The genealogy in Mathew's Gospel has striking meaning. The Apostle followed the usual Jewish practice of listing the lineage of a person to authenticate the person's ancestry. The words in this list confirm that Jesus was of the line of David and therefore fulfilled one of the primary requirements for the Messiah. The confirmation of Jesus as son of David and son of Abraham supported the contention that Jesus is the Christ, the promised Messiah of God.

The genealogy, by mentioning women—including Gentile women and some with a shady background—stresses that in the message of the gospel, God would reach out to all people. The Gentiles and sinful persons would become God's people. The gospel of Christ centers on the all-embracing love of God that will reach all humans and is unwilling that any perish (1 Timothy 2:1–6). Further, God can call and use the services of persons who have taken wrong directions. God can cleanse and use people whose wrong lives would turn away many who claim to have a relationship with him. Christians and churches should allow God's Spirit to develop within them the intense love for and desire to reach those who often are rejected by religious groups.

In these words of genealogy, we learn that God desires the salvation of people who are classed as outcasts and the despised in society. The barriers that have grown up due to human sinfulness are torn away by the final completion of God's plan through Israel and through Christ.

A question for Christians today is how well we incorporate this commitment to reach out to the oppressed and marginalized of society. Christians and churches today must move beyond merely ministering to these oppressed and tried peoples and must find ways to exalt them and affirm their tremendous value in God's plan. We must become willing to reach out in genuine desire to contribute to their salvation and new life in Christ.

Each Christian and each church should find those unsaved and unchurched people who need God and the ministry of the churches. How can you find and reach out to these needy people?

TEACHING PLANS

Teaching Plan—Varied Learning Activities

Connect with Life

1. Invite the class to think for a moment about their family trees, including some of the ancestors they know about. Ask, *Does anyone have any famous or "colorful" relatives?* Take responses, and then ask, *How do we feel about our distinguished relatives? How do we feel about relatives who were "black sheep"? Why do we feel that way?* Allow a few moments for discussion. Then ask, *What do we learn about ourselves or about other people from a family tree or genealogy?*

2. Say, *Matthew had a purpose when he wrote the genealogy of Jesus into his Gospel. Let's study it together to see why.*

Guide Bible Study

3. Read aloud Matthew 1:1–17. Instruct the class to count the generations, as mentioned in verse 17. Ask, *Why do you think Matthew called attention to Abraham and David?*

4. Point out that the Hebrew term *messiah* (or *christos* in Greek) means *anointed,* and could refer to prophets, priests, or kings. Ask, *In what ways was Jesus a prophet? a priest? a king?*

5. In advance, enlist four people to research the stories of Tamar (Genesis 38), Rahab (Joshua 2:1–21; 5:22–25), Ruth (Ruth 1), and the wife of Uriah (2 Samuel 11) and present a report no longer than

one to two minutes each. (You could also simply review the information in the *Study Guide* and "Bible Comments" in this *Teaching
Guide*.) At the conclusion of the reports ask, *Which of these women
surprises you most to be included in Jesus' genealogy? Which of these
women would you want to include in your family tree? Why?*

6. Note that some of the people mentioned in Jesus' ancestry were
   declared to be wicked (for example, Ahaz, Matt. 1:9; 2 Chronicles
   28:19; Manasseh, Matt. 1:10; 2 Kings 21:11; Amon, Matt. 1:10;
   2 Chron. 33:21–23). Ask, *Why do you think Matthew included these
   people in Jesus' genealogy? What can we conclude about the influence of previous generations on an individual? How does this provide
   you with hope for yourself and for other people you care about?*

Encourage Application

7. Make two columns on the markerboard, labeling one "Similarities"
   and the other "Differences." Invite the group to think about the
   people in your Bible study class. Then lead the class to list some
   of the ways most of you are the same and some of the ways you
   are different. Then ask, *In what ways do our likenesses enhance
   our relationships and make our class stronger and more effective?
   What about our differences?* Allow some time for discussion. Then
   ask, *Do these likenesses and differences also strengthen the body of
   Christ? How?*

8. Call attention to this *Study Guide* statement (under the heading, "What's in a Name?"): "Matthew's Gospel spoke to a church
   that needed to see a bigger picture of God's love and to remember
   that Christ was the hope for the whole world." Then refer to this
   statement under "Implications and Applications": "Our job is not
   to draw lines of exclusion. Rather it is to imagine God at work in
   the lives of people who are different from ourselves. These people
   may be crucial to the work of God's kingdom." Ask the class to
   brainstorm examples of ways people "draw lines of exclusion" in
   a church. Write the thoughts on a markerboard, and then ask for
   some specific suggestions to avoid or remedy the actions or attitudes mentioned. Also ask, *How do you think God is at work in the
   lives of people who are different from ourselves?*

9. Divide the class into small groups of six or fewer people. Have each group read the small article "What Would Happen in Your Church?" Instruct each group to pretend they were a committee selected by the minister to make sure the young woman in the case study was accepted by the church and then enabled to find her gifts of service and to make a difference. *What specific actions would they advise for the church?*

10. Conclude with prayer that each individual, the whole class, and the entire church may be able to embrace and share Christ with other people regardless of any perceived differences.

Teaching Plan—Lecture and Questions

Connect with Life

1. Lead the class to brainstorm some reasons ancient Israelites included genealogies in their Scriptures. (You may need to begin by explaining what a genealogy is. Refer to the information in the small article, "Biblical Genealogies.")

2. Say, *These days, many people introduce themselves in the workplace with a professional resumé or curriculum vitae. How is a resumé similar to and different from a genealogy? What does a resumé tell about a person that is not evident in a genealogy, and vice versa?*

Guide Bible Study

3. Read through Matthew 1:1–17. Ask, *Why does this passage emphasize Abraham and David in 1:1 and 1:17?* (As a hint, call for a volunteer to read aloud Genesis 12:1–3 and 2 Samuel 7:8–16.)

4. Using information from the *Study Guide* and from "Bible Comments" in this *Teaching Guide*, present information on some of the people mentioned in the genealogy in Matthew 1:1–17. Focus especially on the women—Tamar, Rahab, Ruth, and the wife of Uriah. Add other information, as time permits, about the character of some of the other kings, such as Rehoboam, Hezekiah,

Manasseh, or Josiah. Stress that both good and wicked people show up in this list of generations.

5. Say, *This text is mostly about bloodlines and family relationships. How does Christianity redefine the family of God?* (See Luke 8:21; Romans 8:14; Galatians 3:26.) Then ask, *Whom do you view as part of your Christian family, but not your biological family?*

Encourage Application

6. Lead a discussion using questions 1, 3, and 5 in the *Study Guide* plus questions such as these:

   a. Do you feel as if you are part of the family of God? Why?

   b. What does it take to make one feel like family?

   c. How can we help other believers feel like family?

   d. What are some advantages to being part of a family? Do these advantages apply to being part of the Christian family? How?

   e. When Christians talk about sharing Christ with all people, what pops into your mind with the phrase *all people*?

   f. What does this passage suggest about who is to be included in God's family?

   g. What can we do to reach out to people who seem different from us?

7. Refer to the small article "What Would Happen in Your Church?" in the *Study Guide.* Enlist someone to read it aloud. Invite the class to discuss what would happen if this occurred at their own church. Continue by asking, *In what ways would our church be effective in welcoming and encouraging the young woman? In what ways does our church need to improve the way we affirm and encourage people? What are some things we could do in our Bible study class?*

NOTES

1. Unless otherwise indicate, all Scripture translations in lessons 1–5 are from the New International Version.

FOCAL TEXT
Matthew 1:18–25

BACKGROUND
Matthew 1:18–25

MAIN IDEA
Jesus, who is God with us,
came to bring salvation.

QUESTION TO EXPLORE
What does Jesus' birth mean?

TEACHING AIM
To lead adults to explain
the meaning of Jesus' birth
and to testify of how it
speaks to them personally

LESSON TWO
*Jesus—Savior—
God with Us*

UNIT ONE
Hope in Jesus' Birth

BIBLE COMMENTS

Understanding the Context

Matthew continued his effort to show that Jesus Christ fulfills the Old Testament hopes for the Messiah. He followed the genealogy in the first part of this chapter and continued with revelations concerning the birth and childhood of Jesus. Matthew used strong language to show that Jesus fulfilled the Old Testament prophecies. The Gospel writer definitely showed that the preparation for the ministry of Jesus corresponded to the Old Testament patterns.

Matthew contended that both Jesus' origin and the giving of the name Jesus indicated that Jesus is the Messiah. The genealogy indicates that Jesus was and is the son of David. Matthew 1:18–25 relates to scriptural proof of Jesus' messiahship. These verses contain one of Matthew's ten formula-quotations, that is, those expressions such as "this came about to fulfill what was said" (see a listing of these in "Understanding the Context" in lesson one).

The account of Jesus' birth to Mary, who had not experienced sexual intercourse, fulfilled Scripture. We give no credence to the theories that Matthew used stories from his imagination to support his view of Jesus' divine nature. That these accounts are part of the inspired text of Scripture attests to their accuracy. The Christians of Matthew's day already knew that Jesus was born in a miraculous way, that he was taken to Egypt, that there was a slaughter of children, and that Jesus' home was in Nazareth.

Old Testament prophecies can be understood as promises God makes to his people. Many of these promises were fulfilled close to the time at which they were made. For example, the promise of a suffering servant in Isaiah 52—53 may have been fulfilled through either a suffering prophet or an exiled nation. God was acting to deliver his people in Old Testament times. Old Testament prophecies may well have had a historical referent for that day but later could have a fuller meaning to bring God's truth to a new level.

These passages reveal that Jesus is the person born to be Savior of humankind. His origin, his name, and his conception as a result of the work of the Holy Spirit reinforced Matthew's teaching that Jesus Christ was the Messiah and Savior for all people.

Interpreting the Scriptures

The Origin of Jesus, the Messiah (1:18–19)

1:18. Matthew declared the facts relating to the birth of Jesus Christ by pointing to the miraculous nature of Jesus' conception. Jesus' mother, Mary, was pledged to be married to Joseph, the normal custom of marriage that was operative at the time of Jesus' birth. In the Jewish custom, a woman often was promised to a man in what was known as an engagement. The parents of the couple, through the services of a matchmaker, sealed the union. The Jews thought marriage to be far too serious to leave it to human passion and youthful decision.

A second step in the marriage process, the betrothal ("pledged to be married"), ratified the engagement. The woman could break the engagement, but once the couple began the yearlong betrothal, the agreement could be terminated only by divorce. The couple was considered and called husband and wife but did not consummate the marriage by sexual intercourse. If the husband died during the betrothal period, the woman was known as a widow.

The third stage, the marriage proper, took place at the end of the year of betrothal. At this time, the husband took the woman to his house, and normal marital relationships were commenced.

Matthew described precisely the Jewish practice of the period at the time Jesus was born. All Jews of that day would have understood that during this year of betrothal, Joseph and Mary would not have come together sexually.

The conception of Jesus by a virgin mother without the agency of Joseph is clearly stated in this section. The teaching of the miraculous conception of Jesus did not grow out of the accounts from other religions of the birth of human children to gods. Matthew announced that Jesus was conceived by a virgin and says little of the way the event happened.

The conception was "through the Holy Spirit." In Jewish understanding, the Spirit of God was active in creation and re-creation. The Spirit brings God's truth to humans and allows humans to comprehend it. The Spirit alone can recreate humans when they have lost the way. In the birth of Jesus, the Spirit of God was operative in a way never before experienced in this world.

The words of verse 18 indicate that the virginal conception of Jesus allowed the Messiah to be totally God and totally human. As fully God, Jesus was able to pay the eternal price of our sins (see 1:21). As fully human, Jesus could be our adequate representative and substitutionary sacrifice.

1:19. Joseph, however, knew nothing of the Sprit's working within Mary. Her pregnancy led him to believe that she had been unfaithful. Old Testament law (Deuteronomy 22:13–21) set the penalty for unfaithfulness as death by stoning. By the time of Jesus' birth, however, divorce based on the teachings of Deuteronomy 24:1–4 had become the more standard practice.

Because Joseph was a "righteous man," that is, a just or law-abiding man, he turned away from a public accusation of sinfulness and an open trial that would have resulted in public disgrace. He elected for the permitted alternative of a private (settlement out of court) divorce before two witnesses. He opted for this quiet way.

The Name of Jesus, the Messiah (1:20–23)

1:20. God quickly moved to change Joseph's plans. We should honor and respect Joseph on the basis of his decision to accept and follow the will of God in what had to be a difficult and heart-wrenching decision. An angel of the Lord spoke to Joseph in a dream. Such communication was an important means of communication between God and humans in the Old Testament and into the New Testament period (see Genesis 16:11; Matthew 27:19). Angels were, and are, supernatural messengers who spoke to people on God's behalf.

The angel assured Joseph that he could take Mary to his home. This terminology "angel of the Lord," also occurs in Matthew 2:13; 2:19; and 28:2. This instruction from the angel indicated that Joseph should not fear to take the next step in the marriage procedure. Joseph accepted the angel's explanation that Mary had conceived supernaturally. The God who created the world can bring about such miracles. The angel addressed Joseph as "son of David," thus reminding Joseph of his place in the messianic line and that he should go on with the plan to marry Mary. In this way, Jesus would legally be the "son of David."

1:21. Joseph received instruction to name the child *Jesus*. The name *Jesus* (in Hebrew *Yeshua*) means *Yahweh (God) is salvation* or *the Lord saves*. This promised Messiah would not liberate Israel from its enemies but would bring spiritual salvation by removing the alienation from God that their sins had established (see Psalm 138:7). God instructed Joseph that the child should be named Jesus because he would save his people from their sins. For "people" in this verse, Matthew used the term *laos*, a term that related to the chosen people. Matthew 28:19 indicates a wider application for Jesus' saving activity than for the one people, the Jews.

1:22–23. Matthew turned to the first of his formula quotations from the Old Testament, "All this took place to fulfill. . . ." He referenced Isaiah 7:14. Matthew employed the Greek word *parthenos*, "virgin," while the Hebrew word in Isaiah 7:14 is the word *alma* (young woman).[1] The prophecy in Isaiah relates the promise to the immediate historical situation during the reign of Ahaz. The promise to Ahaz assured him God would deliver Judah from the Assyrians by the time a then-pregnant woman gave birth and that child could distinguish between right and wrong. Matthew's use of Isaiah 7:14 emphasizes the larger fulfillment in the virgin birth of Jesus.

Jesus was the ultimate fulfillment of God's promise. He truly is Immanuel. Ascribing the name Immanuel ("God with us") to Jesus further establishes that Matthew taught that Jesus was and is the Messiah of God. Matthew later promised that Jesus would continue to be "with us" to the end of the age (28:20).

Joseph's Obedience to the Angel (1:24–25)

When Joseph awoke, he followed the instruction of the angel. He completed the betrothal phase of the marriage by taking Mary to his home as his wife.

Matthew explicitly stated that although they were legally husband and wife, they had "no union," that is, sexual intercourse, until after the birth of Jesus. The expression "until after" indicates that sexual union did not happen until after the birth. After Jesus' birth, Joseph and Mary had other children in the normal way (see Matt. 12:46, 47).

Focusing on the Meaning

The New Testament proclaims that Jesus is the promised Messiah. Jesus fulfills the Old Testament prophecies concerning the Messiah. Jesus is God with us, the Savior who will save his people from their sins. We know that God has come to us in Christ and his salvation is always near.

The meaning in the passage is clear. In Jesus, the almighty Creator is "God with us." Jesus, who is fully God and fully human, enables sinful humans to come to God, receive the forgiveness of sins, and have eternal life.

The teaching of the miracle of the conception of Jesus is a basic biblical teaching and should remain a vital belief of Christians today. Believers should not allow the questions and doubts of some to lower their acceptance of this clear teaching of Scripture.

The teachings in these verses likewise show that Jesus Christ is Messiah, not just for the Jewish people, but also for all people. Matthew provides the most comprehensive statement of God's desire that his people take his message to all in Matthew 28:16–20. The clear teaching of these verses is the importance of a worldwide Christian evangelistic effort.

Because of the assurance that Jesus is Messiah for all peoples, believers today can and should come boldly to God's throne (Hebrews 4:16). Jesus Christ is the One through whom salvation can and will come to believers (John 3:16–21). The account of the birth and naming of Jesus makes clear that the path to God is open and certain. God is with humanity now and until the end of the age.

Joseph and Mary are tremendous examples of obedience to God under difficult circumstances. Mary accepted the angel's announcements with praise and willingness to be used in God's plan. Joseph, after hearing the angel's assurance, obediently moved to complete the marriage process and to accept the responsibility of caring for the son.

Obedience in difficult times should be the path for all Christians. Christians should seek to obey God in every circumstance without fear of the opinions of others. What God indicates as his will becomes the imperative path for believers.

TEACHING PLANS

Teaching Plan—Varied Learning Activities

Connect with Life

1. Invite the class to tell about amusing names they have heard over the years in which someone's name related to his or her vocation. (For example, Dr. Sharp, the surgeon; Mr. Baker, the pastry chef; Mr. Boring, the teacher, and so on.) After a few minutes, ask whether names like these can be self-fulfilling, that is, whether someone's name can influence his or her life, and why.

2. Next, state that in the Bible, people are frequently given a name that reflects their life situation or some kind of prophecy. Ask whether anyone can think of examples. (Hint: Genesis 16:11; 35:10; Hosea 1:9; Acts 4:36.) Say, *Today we will study about Joseph and what he was told about the coming birth of Jesus, including the name the baby was to be given. The Bible says that the baby was given "the name Jesus, because he will save his people from their sins" (Matt. 1:21). The name means "The Lord saves." We will also talk about the name "Immanuel," which means "God with us," and how Jesus as God with us makes a difference in our lives.*

Guide Bible Study

3. Invite someone to read Matthew 1:18–25 while class listens for the various elements in Joseph's experience. After the reading, ask, *Do you have any experience with a dream that you believed was a special kind of message? Do you think it was God communicating with you? Why?*

4. Divide into small groups (no more than six people in each) or pairs. Refer to the *Study Guide* section "An Agonizing Change of Plans." Provide paper and markers and instruct the groups to outline, draw, or diagram the various alternatives Joseph had when he

discovered his betrothed (that is, his fiancée, Mary) was pregnant. Encourage the groups to note the personal, spiritual, or social forces that might have influenced his dilemma. Call for presentations of the diagrams.

5. State that the angel of the Lord told Joseph that the child to be born would "save his people from their sins." Ask, *What do you think this meant to Joseph?* Then refer to verse 23, especially the title "Immanuel"—which means, "God with us." Ask the same question, *What do you think this meant to Joseph?* Continue by asking, *How do you think these two ideas might be connected—Jesus as "God with us" and Jesus saving the people from their sins?*

Encourage Application

6. Ask the class to return to their small groups or pairs. Instruct each group to review today's Bible text and the *Study Guide* and then write a monologue for Joseph reflecting what he thought and felt about his betrothal to Mary, the situation with her surprise pregnancy, and the dream/vision of the angel. Receive reports.

7. Refer to the *Study Guide* section titled "The One Who Will Save You (1:20–23)," the paragraph that begins, "The solutions to our most difficult problems. . . ." Ask the class to note the prayer in italics, *"God, do you see this as I'm seeing it? Am I missing what is really going on here? Am I too close to the pain to see the promise of your presence?"* Have the class suggest some ways the Lord might bring about a change in a person's perspective and some examples of when they believe that has happened to them.

8. Review the small article titled "What Would Jesus Do—with You?" in the *Study Guide*. Lead the class in discussing and defining what each of these actions might look like in our lives. Ask what else they might add to the list.

9. Refer to this statement in the *Study Guide* under "Implications and Actions": "Our lives are not to be cul-de-sacs of Jesus' saving presence, but thoroughfares to the hearts of people who need to know they are not alone." Invite the group to turn to two other people

and discuss in threes how we can demonstrate the presence of Jesus in our lives.

10. Point to the title of the lesson and invite the class to reflect on the meaning for their lives of the titles "Savior" and "God with us." Close with a prayer thanking God for sending Jesus Christ to be our "Savior" and "God with us."

Teaching Plan—Lecture and Questions

Connect with Life

1. Write the words "Save" and "Saved" on the markerboard. Ask the class to suggest as many meanings as possible. Jot the ideas on the markerboard. After a few minutes, state: *The name "Jesus" can mean "Yahweh will save."* Then ask, *Which of these meanings of "save" do you think are applicable for the name of our Lord?*

2. Say that today we will talk about Joseph, how he learned about the coming birth of Jesus, and how the prophecy he received that Jesus would be "God with us" gave hope to him and gives hope to all who have faith in Christ.

Guide Bible Study

3. Read Matthew 1:18–25 aloud. Refer to the *Study Guide* and "Bible Comments" in this *Teaching Guide* to explain the marriage customs of first-century Palestine. Ask, *What do you think were the advantages or disadvantages of this process of betrothal and marriage?*

4. Invite the class to volunteer information or present your own ideas about why Mary's pregnancy would have been such a problem for Joseph (and Mary). You may want to refer to Exodus 20:14 and/or Leviticus 20:10.

5. Point out that the *Study Guide* states under the heading "The One Who Will Save You (1:20–23)," "He [Joseph] would do so [divorce Mary] quietly and privately, but the decision would not quiet the

turmoil in his spirit." Ask, *Why do you think Joseph would have continued to be upset about his decision?*

6. Ask, *Why would Joseph be afraid to take Mary as his wife? How does a sense of God's presence—or a lack of such a sense—influence our thoughts and actions in difficult times?*

7. Use information in the *Study Guide* and "Bible Comments" in this *Teaching Guide* to explain Matthew 1:21–25 further as needed.

Encourage Application

8. Invite the class to comment on the meaning for their lives of the phrases "he will save his people from their sins" and "God with us." Lead the class in a discussion using questions such as: *When do you most sense God's presence—when you are in trouble, or when things seem to be going well? Why? How can a person cultivate the sense of God's presence? Can you remember a time when you were in pain or struggling somehow that you felt God's presence and it was sufficient?* Use the questions from the *Study Guide*, too.

9. Lead the class to imagine and describe what their life would be like if God had not sent Jesus. (Some examples are not having Jesus' teachings or his personal example of ethical loving relationships; relying on human actions to atone for sins; no assurance of eternal life.)

10. Invite comments about what it means to have the Lord's presence, to have Jesus as "God with us." Then ask them to complete the sentence, "Because Jesus is God with us, I have hope that _____." Conclude with prayer.

N O T E S

1. The Septuagint, the Greek translation of the Old Testament, uses *parthenos* in Isaiah 7:14.

FOCAL TEXT
Matthew 2:1–12

BACKGROUND
Matthew 2

MAIN IDEA
The Wise Men's seeking and
worshiping Jesus signifies
that Jesus is for all people
and calls us to reach out to
all people for Jesus' sake.

QUESTION TO EXPLORE
What are we doing about
the New Testament truth
that Jesus is for all people?

TEACHING AIM
To lead the class to identify
ways they will participate
in Jesus' mission for
reaching the people they
may call "foreigners"

LESSON THREE
Coming to Find Jesus

UNIT ONE
Hope in Jesus' Birth

BIBLE COMMENTS

Understanding the Context

In chapter 2, Matthew continued to prepare the stage for the beginnings of Jesus' ministry. In these verses, Matthew wrote of Jesus' birth
in the town of Bethlehem and linked this place to messianic prophecy.
He related the coming of the Magi, philosophers from the East who
came to pay homage to the child and who brought gifts fit for royalty.
Matthew also recounted the terrible deeds of Herod, who allowed his
excessive suspicions and jealousies to drive him to murder the babies
in Bethlehem. This chapter is the only place in the Gospels that tells of
the flight to Egypt, where Joseph found protection for the baby Jesus.
Finally, the chapter reveals how the family returned to Nazareth, where
Jesus would grow into manhood.

This week's text traces several themes in Matthew's presentation of
Jesus. Along with the explanation of the birth in Bethlehem, the chapter
contrasts Herod to Jesus as King of the Jews, Herod's usurpation of the
throne, and his evil acts to hold it. Matthew, throughout his Gospel,
compared Jesus with Moses to show that Jesus was the new Moses. Here
we see the first likeness. Both Jesus and Moses lived in Egypt before
coming into leadership among the world's people. The chapter rein-
forces the tremendous truth that Jesus is Messiah for all people, not just
for the Jews.

An important, although almost totally unrecorded, phase of Jesus'
life took place in Nazareth. These years made up more than ninety per-
cent of Jesus' days on earth. During these years, Jesus learned the life of
a working person. His experiences helped him identify with ordinary
humans and their struggles and molded him in character and knowledge. They enabled him to prepare for the larger task of becoming Savior
as he performed the service of being the oldest child and supporting the
family.

This chapter and the next, which recounts the beginning of Jesus'
ministry, prepare the way for the account of the life and ministry of
Jesus. They also show that Jesus' influence would extend far beyond the
boundaries of Judaism.

Interpreting the Scriptures

From the East to Jerusalem (2:1–8)

2:1. The events chronicled in 2:1–11 happened after the birth of Jesus. We cannot be certain how long after his birth that the Magi arrived. Verse 11 indicates that Mary and Joseph had left the humble place of the birth (see Luke 2:7) and now resided in a house. Jesus was no longer a baby but a child. The verse introduces several characters and places in the story.

First, the place of the birth is the Judean village of Bethlehem which was located some six miles south of Jerusalem. Situated on a limestone hill 2,500 feet high, the area possessed a summit at either end with a hollow, saddle-like area between. In older times, Bethlehem had been known as Ephrath or Ephrathah. The name *Bethlehem* meant *house of bread*, a name made fitting by the fertile land in the area.

This verse introduces the players in the drama—King Herod and the Magi. Herod was half-Jew and half-Idumean. By compromise and moderation, he had so ingratiated himself to the Romans that he ascended to the throne around 37 B.C. He was known as a great builder and at times treated the people kindly. But he had gained the hatred of many Jews by his taxation policies and his conscription of labor. Herod also was intensely paranoid and suspicious of any who might threaten his rule. These failings led him to put to death numerous sons, wives, and others whom he thought were threats to overthrow him. Caesar Augustus is reported to have said that he had rather be Herod's pig than his son. *Pig* and *son* sound similar in Greek pronunciation.

The second group of players was the "Magi, from the East." The word "Magi" describes these men better than either *Wise Men* or *kings*. The Magi were philosophers, astrologers, practitioners of medicine, and magicians. They likely came from Persia. These men practiced fortune-telling and dream interpretation. In early times and at their best, the Magi were respected. They later became known as sorcerers, fortune-tellers, and charlatans. The sorcerer Elymas (Acts 13:6, 8) and Simon Magnus (Acts 8:9, 11) followed the evil ways of the Magi in later days.

2:2. The Magi indicated they were Gentiles by having to ask where they could find the one "born" to be king of the Jews. The Magi arrived from the East and announced they had seen the star of the king of the Jews rising. Attempts to identify the star with astronomical phenomena such as the conjunction of Jupiter and Saturn in AD 7, a comet, or a nova have proved unsatisfying. Matthew seems to indicate that the guiding star was a miraculous and unexplained occurrence. By some miracle, the God of creation led these Gentiles to the place where they could worship the greatest of the miracles, God becoming human to redeem all believing humans. The Magi declared they had come to worship this king.

2:3. Herod proved his lack of knowledge of the Jewish religion by his ignorance of the birthplace of the Messiah. "Disturbed" is too weak a word for Herod's response to the coming of the Magi. The word describes being *terrified* or *tremendously agitated.*

2:4. "All Jerusalem" probably means the religious leaders of the city. Herod had appointed many of these leaders. The terms "chief priests" and "teachers" probably relate to an ad hoc meeting and not an official meeting of the Sanhedrin since Herod was not on good terms with the Jewish court. Herod's question indicated his terror as he asked where the Christ was to be born.

2:5–6. The Jewish leaders answered quickly and directly, pointing to a definite messianic prophecy from Micah 5:2. Matthew quoted freely from the passage in Micah to stress the messianic nature of Christ. He also emphasized the quality of shepherd in the Christ as expressed in 2 Samuel 5:2. Matthew once again used the formula-quotation of "it has been written."

The addition of the words "by no means" shows that the birth of the Christ in Bethlehem transformed Bethlehem from a relatively unimportant town to one of great consequence. The Jews would understand Matthew's use of the Old Testament as he showed that the Christ would rule over Israel as a shepherd.

2:7–8. Verses 7 and 16 demonstrate the evil that motivated Herod and his plans. The king called the Magi *quietly* ("secretly") and enquired about the exact time the Magi had seen the star. Using this ruse would allow the king to target the time of the birth and make plans for his further efforts to eliminate the threat of Christ.

Herod's protestation that he wanted to worship the Christ child was a complete lie. Herod had no plans to worship the child, but only the plan to do away with another threat to his throne. Some have suggested that Herod was too shrewd and cunning to depend on the cooperation of these foreigners and that he may have sent soldiers along with them. At any rate, he sent the Magi on their way to make a careful search for the child and report back to him so he too could "worship."

From Jerusalem to Bethlehem (2:9–11)

2:9. The most natural understanding of the star's movement is that it led the Magi to the place where Joseph, Mary, and the child awaited them. The words "went ahead" could mean that it led them without itself moving, but the addition of the words "it stopped over the place where the child was" suggests actual movement. These words indicate that the family had moved from the place of birth, probably to a house, and that Jesus had grown from a baby to a child. The exact period of time between the birth and the coming of the Magi is not made clear.

The Magi may not have discerned Herod's evil plans at first. Later, though, they followed the guidance of an angel to thwart the evil intentions of the cruel ruler.

2:10. The Magi were filled with joy at seeing the child. Verse 10 indicates they experienced great joy at what they perceived as divine guidance by the star. Divine leadership is ever a matter of great joy.

2:11. On coming to the house, they "saw the child, with his mother, Mary." They worshiped not Mary, but the child. They brought gifts that ordinarily and typically were associated with royalty. Gold has long been the medium of value. Incense and myrrh were fragrant spices often related to royalty. These gifts were deemed worthy for a king (see Psalm 72; Isaiah 60).

The Divine Plan Fulfilled (2:12; see also 2:13–23)

2:12. The Magi received a direct warning from an angel not to return to Herod. They returned home by a different route.

Verses 13–23 complete the account of these events. The angel once again warned Joseph of the danger from Herod, instructing Joseph to take the family to Egypt where they could live among the large group of Jewish exiles there. Matthew also saw this sojourn in Egypt as a fulfillment of prophecy and another linking of the Christ to Moses.

Realizing he had been outwitted by the Magi, Herod attempted to eliminate the threat of the Christ by killing the babies of Bethlehem under two years of age. The number of babies actually killed may have been twenty or more. Whatever the number, the cruelty was intense. Matthew related the sorrow and grief of the mothers of Bethlehem to that of Rachael at Ramah (Jeremiah 31:15).

After Herod's death (around 4 B.C.), the angel again instructed Joseph to take the child back to Nazareth. Matthew does not indicate that Joseph and Mary had come to Bethlehem from Nazareth. The phrase, "he will be called a Nazarene," does not suggest Jesus belonged to the cult by that name but may have stressed his humble beginnings.

Focusing on the Meaning

The coming of Gentile Magi to visit the birthplace of Jesus emphasizes the worldwide nature of God's message. The gift of the Christ goes far beyond a matter only for the Jews. The inclusion of the story of the Magi indicates that God's great plan includes all the peoples of the world. The visit of the philosophers from the East shows the fulfillment of the Old Testament teachings of God's people being a light to all and taking the message of God's love to the ends of the earth (Isaiah 49:6).

A second truth in these verses relates to God's significant care for his people. The angel of the Lord intervened in the family's experience, and God both assured and warned Mary, Joseph, and the Magi. Believers can have full assurance of God's continuing care because the most vicious plans of evil people can never defeat God's plans.

A third important meaning in these passages relates to the imperative of obedience to the leading of God. Joseph and Mary are examples of willingness to follow God's leading even when this leading seems contrary to human reason. Obedience to God is one of the most basic of factors in Christian living and service. When facing difficult decisions, believers should seek God's leading and, in full obedience, follow that leading.

A fourth meaning in the section relates to the joy believers find in obedience to God's leadings. The joy of the Magi led them to bring

LESSON 3: Coming to Find Jesus

gifts to Jesus that were the types given to royalty. The Magi experienced great joy as they realized God's leadership and engaged in deep worship of the child.

A fifth meaning in the story relates to the supernatural workings of God in this world. The announcement to Mary, her conception of the baby in a supernatural way, the assurances given to Joseph, and the guidance to the Magi all indicate the supernatural workings of God. Christians today should accept and affirm the reality of God working supernaturally and expect God to continue working in supernatural ways.

TEACHING PLANS

Teaching Plan—Varied Learning Activities

Connect with Life

1. In advance, ask members to bring ornaments or other decorations in the shape of a star. (You could also collect and bring several examples of your own.) Spend a few minutes on *show-and-tell*. Then ask, *What do stars symbolize?* List responses on a markerboard.

2. Point out this statement in the *Study Guide* under the heading "An Enduring Symbol of Hope": "For them the star was a visible symbol of God's action in history, providing the guidance they needed in their lives." Then say, *Today we will study the Magi and talk about how people of all times and places seek for truth and guidance and how we are to help others, even people different from us, find the truth of Christ.*

Guide Bible Study

3. Enlist someone to read Matthew 2:1–12 aloud while the class listens for the exchange between the Magi and Herod. Then form small groups of no more than six people each. Instruct each group to pretend they are the ancient Magi, preparing to journey by camel

from somewhere around Baghdad to Jerusalem. Each group is to list what they would need to pack for the journey. After a few minutes, instruct the groups to now pretend they are going on a long journey from this church to tell people about Jesus Christ. *What would they pack for this journey?* Allow a few more minutes, and then call for group reports.

4. Create two columns on a markerboard, labeling one "Herod" and the other "Magi." Using the *Study Guide* and the Bible, lead the class to brainstorm ways Herod and the Magi were similar or different in matters such as trust, curiosity, egotism, use of power, reaction to the news of the birth, background, and so on. Write the comparisons/contrasts on the markerboard.

5. Present information from the *Study Guide* and "Bible Comments" on 2:12 in this *Teaching Guide* about the significance of the Magi's gifts. Ask, *What was the best gift you received this past Christmas? What was the best gift you gave?* After several people have responded, ask, *What gifts do you offer to Christ?* Allow some time for thought, and then ask for responses.

6. State that the Magi were seeking truth. Divide into small groups and instruct each group to role play or write a three-minute skit of what they would say to the ancient Magi about Jesus Christ.

Encourage Application

7. Divide into small groups again (perhaps forming groups differently from step 3) and distribute two or three newsmagazines to each group. Invite class members to tear out photos of "foreigners." (Do not give instructions or answer questions about what "foreigners" should mean.) After a few minutes, lead the whole group to analyze their experience with this exercise using questions such as: *Did everyone agree on which were photos of "foreigners"? What did you decide were the criteria for photos of "foreigners"?*

8. Read Acts 1:8. Ask, *How should we interpret "Jerusalem, Judea and Samaria, and the ends of the earth" as we seek to obey Jesus' command today? Should we think strictly of geography, or could we also consider the extent to which the gospel is known or welcomed and embraced?*

9. Divide the group into pairs. Tell each pair to take turns role playing. One partner is to play a friend or co-worker who does not have faith in Christ. Instruct this person to visualize someone they actually know. The other partner is to explain his/her faith in Christ. After several minutes, have the partners reverse roles.

   Conclude with prayer that each person may become more engaged in Jesus' mission for reaching all people.

Teaching Plan—Lecture and Questions

Connect with Life

1. Lead your class to perform the exercise explained in the introductory paragraph of the *Study Guide.* Ask the class to answer this question silently, *What are you seeking at this time in your life?* Then invite volunteers to tell their answers. Lead the class to analyze how many of the answers are oriented toward personal or spiritual growth, being careful not to appear to criticize particular quests.

2. Say, *Most adults find themselves seeking guidance and truth. Today we will study the Magi, scholars from the East who traveled to Jerusalem in search of the king of the Jews. As we study, let's think about our own quest for truth and about other people who seek truth as we do.*

Guide Bible Study

3. Read Matthew 2:1–12. Share information about the Magi and the significance of their gifts using the comments in the *Study Guide* and "Bible Comments" in this *Teaching Guide.* (Stress that the Bible text in Matthew does not elaborate on the details of the Magi or explain the significance of their gifts.) Lead a discussion with questions such as:
   - Why do you think the Magi made the journey to Jerusalem?
   - What risks or hardships might they have encountered on the way?

- How might the journey and their encounter with King Herod and with Joseph, Mary, and Jesus have changed them?
- Do you think the Magi expected to find a baby when they were searching for a king?
- Does the idea that Jesus was a toddler when they found him, and not a newborn in a manger, make a difference in the way you view or understand the story of his birth? Why or why not?

4. Share information about Herod the Great from the *Study Guide* and "Bible Comments" in this *Teaching Guide*. Ask:
   - Does Herod remind you of any other prominent world leaders, past or present?
   - Who, and how?
   - Does great power or wealth make a difference in living a moral life?
   - Does it make a difference in one's inclination to accept Christ as Lord and Savior?
   - Why?

5. State: *The Magi possibly believed that the stars had influence over the world and its people, and they were likely what we would call "pagans." Yet, they came to Jerusalem seeking truth. In what ways can we today relate to non-Christians and their beliefs as we explain the gospel and our own faith?*

Encourage Application

6. Call for volunteers to read Luke 2:29–32; Isaiah 9:1–2; 42:6–7; 49:6. Ask, *What do you think the concept of "light to the Gentiles" meant to Isaiah and Simeon? What does "light to the Gentiles" suggest in our times?* (God's mission to all the world)

7. Return to the answers people thought of during the opening exercise. Ask, *How does your faith in Christ help you with seeking and finding what is important? Who else do you know who may need to seek the same things you seek?* Lead the class in prayer for the people they have identified and for themselves.

FOCAL TEXT
Matthew 4:1–11

BACKGROUND
Matthew 3:1—4:11

MAIN IDEA
Jesus' overcoming temptation shows that in his ministry he would be fully faithful to God's way rather than following the way of worldly selfishness.

QUESTION TO EXPLORE
How are you being tempted today?

TEACHING AIM
To lead adults to identify ways in which Jesus' temptations can be compared to their own and determine how they can overcome temptation as Jesus did

LESSON FOUR
Fully Faithful to God's Way

UNIT TWO
Hope in Jesus' Ministry

BIBLE COMMENTS

Understanding the Context

Matthew, as did Luke, jumped abruptly from the accounts of Jesus' birth to the beginnings of his adult ministry. The Gospel writers treated these thirty silent years with brevity and lack of detail. Luke alone recorded the account of the twelve-year-old Jesus in the temple (Luke 2:41–50) and that "Jesus grew in wisdom, stature, and in favor with God and man" (Luke 2:52).

In Matthew 3:1—4:11, Matthew recorded the direct preparations for Jesus' ministry—John, the forerunner, who baptized (Matthew 3:1–6); the coming of the Jewish leaders and John's denunciation of them (Matt. 3:7–12); and Jesus' acceptance of baptism from John the Baptist (3:13–17). This baptism culminated with the assurance from God to Jesus that he was indeed the Messiah whom God fully supported. God's words from heaven, "This is my Son, whom I love; with him I am well pleased" (3:17), hold definite messianic implications. The first phrase is derived from Psalm 2:7 and the second from Isaiah 42:1.

An important factor in the preparation for Jesus' ministry relates to John's message of baptism. John's unique emphasis differed from the baptism of Gentiles who converted to Jewish religion and from the daily cleansing rituals of the monks at the Qumran community, with whom John may have had contact. John's message was *repent* because the "kingdom of heaven," that is, the kingdom of God, was near.

Jesus accepted baptism in the river but not because he needed to repent of wrongdoing. His statement that he did not need baptism in relation to sin but in order to fulfill all righteousness explained his reason for being baptized. To complete "all righteousness" meant everything that forms any part in a relationship of obedience to God.

Too, Jesus did not become Son of God at his baptism. The baptism launched Jesus on his mission for which he had prepared and which followed closely the prophecies of the Messiah in Old Testament teaching. The preparation for his ministry will be completed in the testing in the wilderness that Matthew recounts in 4:1–11.

Interpreting the Scriptures

The Setting of the Event (4:1)

The word "then" indicates that these events came directly after Jesus' baptism and after the assurances God had given him of his messianic nature. Such trials often follow high spiritual experiences as God's people, after some high spiritual victory, are immediately subject to a renewed attack from Satan by way of trials or temptations (see Elijah in 1 Kings 19:1–18 and Paul in Romans 7:14–25).

The same Spirit that had anointed Jesus in Matthew 3:16 now led him to a place of temptation. The Spirit, however, did not tempt Jesus. The temptations came by way of the devil, or Satan. The "wilderness" is probably the same region as that mentioned in Matthew 3:1 as the location from which John came. The desert of Judea is the land that drops steeply down from the Judean hills to the Dead Sea. While this area is not all a desert, it is a region that offers only rough pasture. The wilderness location recalls the wanderings of the people of Israel and their failure. Jesus would succeed as the true representative and fulfillment where Israel had failed (Deuteronomy 8:2).

The name "devil" in Greek means *accuser*, as does Satan in Hebrew. The devil is not an enemy that is equal to God but always remains bound by what God permits.

Satan tempted or tested Jesus. The word "tempted" primarily means *tested* in Matthew. Only in 1 Corinthians 7:5 and James 1:13–14 does the word clearly indicate being tempted to wrongdoing. In Matthew 4:1, the term carries both meanings. Satan sought to entice Jesus to do wrong (tempt), but what the devil saw as a temptation, God simultaneously used as a positive test to prove Jesus' faithfulness and his response to his messianic calling.

The event of temptation (or trial) was a crucial preparatory event in the life of Jesus. A different reaction to the experience in the wilderness could have perverted the nature of Jesus' messianic sonship. Satan tempted Jesus to bypass the way of death and sacrifice and fulfill the current desires for a political commander to lead the people out of Roman bondage. Jesus chose to remain faithful to God and God's plan. Compromise would have given victory to Satan, but total faithfulness to God's will brought fulfillment to God's plan for his people.

The First Temptation (4:2–4)

4:2. Jesus followed the Jewish practice of fasting to increase his spiritual receptivity in prayer. Satan used Jesus' resulting physical hunger as an open door for the testing. "Forty days and forty nights" may have meant the actual number of days or it might have meant simply an extended period of time. The phrase likely was intended to link Jesus' temptation to the period of Israel's wanderings for forty years. The hunger of Jesus was real, for the Son of Man was not exempt from the normal human physical needs.

4:3. Matthew referred to the devil by his function, "the tempter." Satan said to Jesus, "If you are the Son of God, tell these stones to become bread." "If" carries the idea of *since*. Satan employed the words from heaven of Matthew 3:17 that Jesus was the Son of God. If stones can become children (Matt. 3:9) and provide water to the people (Exodus 17:6), stones can surely be changed to bread to meet the physical needs of hunger.

4:4. Jesus answered all the temptations with quotations from Deuteronomy. Jesus could have used supernatural powers to produce bread. Later miracles proved he could and showed the act in itself was not wrong (Matt. 14:15–21; 15:32–38). This temptation was for Jesus to use his powers for selfish purposes. As Son of God, Jesus was called to unquestioning obedience to the Father's plan. Quoting Deuteronomy 8:3, Jesus showed his faithfulness to God's way and his rejection of any selfishness. The principle applies not only to Jesus' situation but also to that of any Christian in any age who is tempted to allow physical needs and desires to take priority over spiritual matters.

The Second Temptation (4:5–7)

Satan again began with "if you are the Son of God." He tempted Jesus to throw himself off the highest point in the temple. The pinnacle or highest point of the temple was the small portico or flat-topped corner of Solomon's porch on the southeast corner of the temple complex overlooking the Kidron Valley. Here the height of the building may have been as much as 180 feet from the ground.

Satan again tempted Jesus to perform a spectacular feat that would entice the people to accept him as Messiah without his following the way of suffering. As Son of God, Jesus could claim the absolute protection of God and his angels (Psalm 91). The test called for Jesus to test God as Israel sinfully did at Massah (Exod. 17:2–7). The Son of God must remain in a relationship of trust that needs no test or proof.

Jesus pointed out the wrong in putting God to any test (Deut. 6:16). Jesus would not create some artificial crisis but would live obediently in total trust of the promises of God. Christians today should not deliberately place themselves in danger so as to test God to bring them to safety. We should never attempt to force God to act in some particular way.

The Third Temptation (4:8–10)

4:8–9. The devil took Jesus to a "very high mountain," which probably described a visionary experience. Satan then made the most brazen test of all—he would give Jesus all the kingdoms of the world if only Jesus would worship him. Actually, Satan ultimately did not have the kingdoms of the world to offer. Satan did, however, hold certain domination over the world (Luke 4:6; John 12:31; 1 John 5:19).

This temptation involved seeking political and spiritual power by compromising with Satan. Worshiping Satan was the one requirement that the tempter offered Jesus to receive all the kingdoms of the earth and their splendor.

4:10. Once again, Jesus met the tempter with the words of Scripture. He resisted Satan by sending him away. Jesus quoted Deuteronomy 6:13, which declared the truth that one was to worship the true and living God and no other. Only this God is worthy of worship.

God's Answers (4:11)

The aid that Jesus had refused to obtain by the wrong methods suggested by Satan now came to Jesus through an angel. All the ministries of the angels came legitimately to Jesus after his continuing obedience to the Father. The angels came and attended to him. The form of the word "came" contains the teaching that the angels came and attended Jesus in a repeated or continuing manner.

Jesus passed the tests. His physical hunger was satisfied. He overcame the idea of using his supernatural powers to escape the way of the cross. Jesus remained faithful to the plan of God for the salvation of humankind through the sacrifice of Calvary.

Focusing on the Meaning

This study of the temptations of Jesus is filled with meaning for Christians today. Consider these teachings:

- The temptations of Jesus were real. His human nature experienced physical hunger. Satan tempted Jesus to take the easier way of using spectacular and supernatural means instead of the way of suffering and the cross. While the temptations were real, the Son of God would not fall into wrongdoing.
- Satan is a real person who sends trials and temptations on people. The devil seeks to cause the fall of every human and will use every deception and trick to lure humans to sin. Since the devil tempted Jesus, he surely will tempt every other human— including believers.
- God does not send temptations. Temptations come from Satan. God can, however, turn temptations into trials that will prove the reality of the trust Christians have in the midst of difficulties and enticements to evil.
- Satan often tempts believers to evil and wrong decisions soon after they experience some high spiritual blessing. When great blessings arise, Christians should be on guard. Watchfulness is imperative after great spiritual experiences.
- Christians may be tempted to compromise and take the easier way rather than the difficult way of sacrifice and suffering. Satan will use personal and selfish enticements in his efforts to tempt humans to sin.
- Believers should place obedience to God ahead of every other consideration. The devil will place barriers in the path of Christians who seek to obey God rather than to take what seems an easier way.
- Christians should have faith to the extent that they never need

to test God in the midst of trials. Christians should not devise situations that call for God to answer needs.

- Christians will find that Scripture is a great protection against temptation and a great strength in their struggles against Satan. Scripture hidden in the heart and mind can empower humans to overcome the devil's temptations.

TEACHING PLANS

Teaching Plan—Varied Learning Activities

Connect with Life

1. Distribute several old magazines and invite class members to tear out photos that represent temptations to adults today. Allow several minutes, and then ask what they found. Ask whether there are other common temptations for which they did not find a photograph. Finally, instruct the class to think of one or more of these that are temptations for them personally. Then say, *Today we will see that even Jesus was tempted. Let's see what we can learn about resisting temptation by studying Jesus' example.*

Guide Bible Study

2. Read the background passage, Matthew 3:1–17. Call attention to the distinctive dress and diet of John the Baptizer. Ask, *Why do you think Matthew included these details in his account?*

3. Invite someone to read Matthew 4:1–4, and encourage the class to listen for what they think the temptation was about. Receive responses, and then use the information from the *Study Guide* and other sources to explain the temptation further. Emphasize that Jesus' first temptation dealt with becoming a leader by meeting people's physical needs. Ask, *Can you think of any world leaders,*

past or present, who have gained power by providing for people's physical needs? Is this a bad or a good thing to do? Why?

4. Enlist someone to read Matthew 4:5–7 and another person to read 4:8–11. Encourage the class to listen for what these temptations were about. Receive responses. Note that in the second exchange, both Satan and Jesus quoted Scripture. Ask, *What do you think is erroneous about Satan's application of Scripture in this passage? In what ways can people apply Scripture erroneously? How can we guard against such wrong applications?*

5. Divide into two or more groups of no more than six people each. Tell each group to act out a short skit of Matthew 4:1–11 that they could present to high school or college students using words and ideas that are meaningful to young people. Allow about five minutes and then call for performances.

6. Ask, *How did Jesus use Scripture to respond to Satan as he resisted the temptations? How can Scripture help us resist temptation?* Then ask, *What are some passages that come to mind that you have found useful in resisting temptation?* Write suggestions on the markerboard, and invite the class to make notes for themselves to put in their Bibles. (For example, use the three passages Jesus used in Matthew 4:1–11. Ask the class how each passage can help with temptations they and other people often face.)

Encourage Application

7. Write the following references on the markerboard, or print them on slips of paper and distribute them to the class: 1 Corinthians 6:18; 1 Timothy 6:9–11; 2 Timothy 2:22; James 4:7. Invite volunteers to read each passage aloud while the rest of the class follows in their Bibles. Then ask, *What temptations are noted in the first three passages? What do you see as the advice for one who is tempted by them? How does the James passage add to our understanding? What does it mean to "flee" from temptation, and how do people like us do it?*

8. Invite someone to read or summarize the small article "Temptation" in the *Study Guide*. Call for comments about how these thoughts can help in dealing with temptation.

9. Review the photographs and other temptations mentioned from the opening activity. Encourage each person to think of a time when he or she failed to resist temptation. Say, *Looking back at that experience, and knowing what you know now, what would you do differently to resist it? How does Jesus' experience help you?*

Teaching Plan—Lecture and Questions

Connect with Life

1. Using a markerboard to list the responses, invite your class to brainstorm some of the "temptations" common to adults like them. After a few minutes generating the list, ask members to consider silently which of these are personal temptations. Then say, *Today we will see that even Jesus was tempted. Let's see what we can learn about resisting temptation by studying Jesus' example.*

Guide Bible Study

2. Refer to and summarize the background passage, Matthew 3:1–17. Ask, *Do you think that being baptized as a Christian is helpful in dealing with temptation? Why or why not? How can recalling our baptism be helpful in resisting temptation?*

3. Invite a volunteer to read Matthew 4:1–4 while the class listens for the temptation Jesus faced and how he responded. Call for responses. Emphasize that the text states that Jesus was hungry. Lead a short discussion with questions such as these: *Does being hungry make people more vulnerable to temptation? Are there different types of "hunger"? Are there different ways of dealing with various kinds of hunger?*

4. Enlist someone to read Matthew 4:5–7. Ask, *What do you think would have happened if Jesus had leapt from the top of the temple and been rescued by angels? What does it mean to put the Lord to the test? What are some ways people put the Lord to the test today?*

5. Tell the class to read Matthew 4:8–11 silently. Ask, *Do you think the devil would have been able to give the kingdoms of the world and their splendor to Jesus? What does your answer say about the temptation of material wealth and power in today's world?*

6. Point out that Jesus frequently quoted Scripture. Ask, *What value is there to being able to quote Scripture? How can Christians avoid applying Scripture incorrectly?*

   State that in order to quote Scripture, one must either carry a Bible at all times or memorize Scripture. Call for suggestions on how to memorize Scripture effectively. You may want to prepare some answers of your own in advance. Lead the class to memorize together the three Scriptures Jesus quoted in Matthew 4:4, 7, 10 ("Man does not live on bread alone, but on every word that comes from the mouth of God." "Do not put the Lord your God to the test." "Worship the Lord your God, and serve him only.")

7. Explain that the Greek term used for "temptation" in this passage is sometimes translated as "trial" (see James 1:2) and can carry the idea of *testing* or *proving* oneself. Ask, *Have you ever been in a circumstance in which you "proved" yourself by resisting temptation? How else can you relate the ideas of testing, trials, and temptation?* (See the small article, "Temptation," in the *Study Guide*.)

8. Refer the class to items 1 and 4 in "Implications and Actions" in the *Study Guide*. Lead the class to consider how temptation relates to major life decisions as well as to daily challenges. Ask, *Are temptations we face regarding major life decisions different from temptations we face in our daily circumstances? Why or why not?*

Encourage Application

9. Direct attention to the questions at the end of the *Study Guide* lesson. Lead the class to consider questions 1 and 2, inviting responses after each. Then direct attention to questions 3 and 4 and allow time for the group to consider each question silently.

MAIN IDEA
Jesus changed people's lives
as they responded to his
proclamation of the kingdom
of heaven in word and deed.

QUESTION TO EXPLORE
In what ways do you yet need
to respond to Jesus' ministry?

TEACHING AIM
To lead adults to evaluate their
response to Jesus' ministry
in light of the response of
the people of Jesus' day and
decide on how they will allow
Jesus to change their lives

LESSON FIVE
The Dawning Light

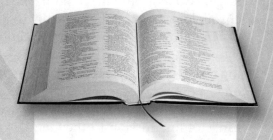

UNIT TWO
Hope in Jesus' Ministry

BIBLE COMMENTS

Understanding the Context

This passage contains the part of Matthew's introduction (Matthew 4:12–16) that specifically introduces the Gospel's sections that describe Jesus' ministry (Matt. 4:17—16:20). Matthew continued to declare that Jesus is the royal Messiah who has fulfilled the messianic promises of Scripture.

The Gospel writer mentioned the rejection of Jesus and the hostility he would face. He established that Jesus was the coming One, the promised Messiah, who would combine the roles of Son and Servant, and the One who would never use his powers to circumvent the suffering of Jesus on the cross. This overall passage reveals how Jesus delivered the message of God by both word and deed.

Matthew indicated that Jesus changed both the location and the style of his ministry. He relocated to Capernaum and turned from a baptizing work (John 3:22–23; 4:1–2) along the Jordan River to one of proclaiming the good news and healing people. The town of Capernaum would provide an effective base from which Jesus and his disciples could continue his intended ministries.

The second part of this lesson's text begins the two main sections of Matthew's story. He began each section with the words, "from that time on, Jesus began to . . ." (Matt. 4:17 and 16:21). Matthew 4:17 begins the largest of the main divisions of the Gospel. Matthew alternated between large blocks of discourse and narrative. The material is organized both chronologically and thematically so as to achieve Matthew's objectives.

In the remaining parts of this section (4:17—16:20), Matthew described the essence of Jesus' preaching and teaching (chapters 5—7) and his healing ministries (chapters 8—9). In chapters 10—12, Matthew concentrated on responses to Jesus and his disciples. Matthew 13:1—16:20 recounts the growing opposition to Jesus, Jesus' teaching in parables, and the beginnings of his mission to the Gentiles. The section speaks to Christians today in regard to the imperative of responding to Christ's call.

Matthew shows how Jesus began his public ministry as he became the dawning light to guide people to God and change the lives of those who trusted him.

Interpreting the Scriptures

The text for today's lesson indicates the content of Jesus' message, his calling of disciples, his proclamation and healing efforts, and the responses of the people to him.

Proclaiming the Message of Jesus (4:12–17)

4:12–13. Jesus heard about the imprisonment of John the Baptist, who had been arrested by Herod. Herod later had John beheaded because of the preacher's denunciation of Herod's marriage to Herodias, the wife of Herod's brother, Philip (14:1–12). Jesus left Judea and returned to Galilee. He soon left Nazareth and settled in Capernaum. Only Matthew recorded that Capernaum became the base for his ministry.

Capernaum was a larger, busier town than Nazareth and therefore more strategic for Jesus' ministries. His leaving Nazareth may have indicated a rejection of him there. Several times the Gospel indicates Jesus withdrew because of official hostility (2:12, 22; 12:14–15; 14:13; 15:21).

Capernaum was located on the edge of the Sea of Galilee. "Sea" should be understood more as a lake, the term Luke always used for the Sea of Galilee. It is an oval-shaped body that is wider at the top than the bottom. It measures thirteen miles from north to south and about eight miles across. Although small, the lake was the source of abundant fish in Jesus' day.

Matthew obviously considered the fact that Capernaum was in the region inhabited by the tribes of Zebulun and Naphtali to be important. This led him to see Jesus' fulfillment of Old Testament prophecy.

4:14–16. Matthew quoted rather freely the passage of Isaiah 9:1–2. The area of Capernaum was "the way to the sea, along [*on the other side of*] the Jordan." Invaders who had often come into Galilee tended to follow this path.

The area is further described as "Galilee of the Gentiles." In Jesus' day, even more than in Isaiah's, more Gentiles than Jews inhabited the land of Galilee. Galilee, a fertile section of the region, was heavily populated. Its Hebrew name came from the word for circle and stemmed from the fact that Galilee was circled by Gentiles—the Phoenicians to the west, the Syrians to the north and east, and the Samaritans to the south. Successive movements of populations and invasions had produced a large Gentile population.

Further, the people of Galilee were widely known for being open to new ideas, fond of innovations, and disposed to change. They held honor in high regard. The characteristics of the Galileans were such as to make them fertile ground for the new message that Jesus would proclaim.

The word "people" is the word that commonly indicated the nation Israel. Jesus would direct his ministry first to Israel but would enlarge his focus to all humanity. The scriptural phrases "living in darkness" and "seen a great light" refer to those who live in ignorance and disobedience of God as differentiated from those who lived in the knowledge and obedience to God.

Matthew used the prophecy of Isaiah that promised deliverance to the people after the Assyrian invasion. The deliverance would now be a spiritual salvation. The light for the people comes through the Messiah, who was brought to reality in the birth of the divine child, Jesus (Isaiah 9:6–7). The stage was now set for the beginning of Jesus' ministry.

4:17. Jesus' method of ministry involved heralding and proclaiming the message. He called on all people to repent, turn from their wicked ways, and come to the light of God. The message was one of certainty and authority and was from God himself.

Jesus called the people to reverse their ways of rejecting God and turn to him and his ways. The imperative for this decision was that the kingdom or reign of God had actually arrived. The kingdom of heaven is the same as the kingdom of God. God had entered history in Jesus Christ. It was imperative for people to choose the right side and the correct direction.

Responding to the Call of Jesus (4:18–22)

4:18–20. Jesus encountered two men, "Simon called Peter and his brother Andrew," who worked as fishermen along the lake. Jesus called these working men to become his disciples. The text indicates they were in the process of casting their nets into the water. Matthew stresses the immediacy of their response. "At once" they put down their nets and followed Jesus.

The basic meaning of a disciple is one who follows a teacher and becomes an adherent of the teacher's ideas and concepts. A disciple becomes an intimate companion. Jesus called these men to "follow him" and become "fishers of men." Jesus did not imply that the method of seeking followers as fishers of men would involve anything deceptive, seductive, or harmful. He indicated that as fishermen seek to gather fish from the lake, so the disciples would gather other followers who would accompany Jesus.

4:21–22. Continuing his journey around the lake, Jesus encountered two other fishermen, James and John, sons of Zebedee. Jesus extended the same call to these men as he did to Peter and Andrew. Matthew declared that they "immediately" left their nets and followed Jesus. The words translated "at once" (4:20) and "immediately" (4:22) are exactly the same word.

The Ministries of Jesus: Teaching, Proclaiming, and Healing (4:23–24)

4:23. On several occasions, Mathew included short summaries of events in Jesus' ministry. Verse 23 is one such summary. He indicated that Jesus left the private lakeside setting and began a public ministry, preaching in open places and visiting the synagogues of the Jews. This ministry was centered "throughout" Galilee. Jesus directed his message first to the Jewish segment of the mixed population in Galilee. Later chapters show, however, that Jesus healed Gentiles during this ministry (8:5–13; 15:21–28).

Jesus' ministries are summarized under four categories: preaching (heralding or publicly proclaiming) the good news (gospel) of the kingdom; teaching in the synagogues (see Luke 4:16); supernaturally healing various types of illness; and calling people to commitment to his kingdom. Preaching or proclaiming relates to the uncompromising announcement of the certainties of God's message while teaching relates to explaining the meaning and significance of these truths.

Jesus healed "every disease and sickness among the people." The word "every" means all kinds of ailments and not every single illness. This healing should be seen as the operation of supernatural power as the power of the kingdom was brought into operation in direct contact with the needs and pains of people.

4:24. The word about Jesus spread to other regions, especially Syria, which lay to the north and east of Galilee. The emphasis once again is on a variety of ailments that Jesus healed. The sicknesses healed included people in severe pain, people having seizures (probably epilepsy), and people who were paralyzed. In addition, Matthew mentioned those who were demonized. Scripture uses the idea of "demon-possessed" to refer to people who were troubled or even controlled by demons. The problem related to an evil spirit taking control of a person, and then acting and speaking through that person. Christians today should not consider demonic activity as only a matter of the past or the view of unsophisticated people. Satan exists and acts today. Much of his activity is through the evil spirits or demons. Jesus had and has power over Satan and the demons. He can empower Christians today to overcome these evil powers.

Response to the Message of Jesus (4:25)

Jesus attracted crowds by heralding the good news and performing the miracles that demonstrated his unique powers. These people came not only from Galilee but also from Judea, Jerusalem, Decapolis (a largely Gentile region east of the Sea of Galilee), and Perea (an area east of the Jordan). Jesus' ministry covered all of Palestine except for Samaria. The text emphasizes that people from all these areas not only listened to Jesus but also responded by following him.

Focusing on the Meaning

Christians today see in these passages the imperative to proclaim the message of good news about Jesus Christ to all people in every region of the world. Jesus began among the Jews but also attracted people from many regions and from among Gentile populations. Knowing that Jesus Christ is the answer that God has for the sins of all people drives believers to carry the good news to those living in darkness and the land of the shadow of death that they might come to the great light that has dawned.

The message in the days of Jesus' ministry in Galilee was "repent." That message remains the message for today. "Repent" means *to turn away from rebellion and disobedience and to obeying and following Jesus.*

The message that Christians today must announce with certainty and with authority is that the "light" has come in Jesus Christ and people must respond individually to this "light." When Christians in faith proclaim the good news about Jesus, people will respond in repentance and faith.

The meaning of these passages also relates to God's call for service from his disciples. The disciples responded "at once." When Jesus calls, his followers should respond immediately. Anything other than following him immediately and fully in service is too little a response.

These passages stress the power of God among people. The message of Jesus Christ calls people to respond. Christians can be certain that people everywhere will accept the good news of Jesus as Savior and Messiah. Christians can be certain, too, of God's continuing power over problems and ailments in human lives. Christians must also, like Jesus, be concerned about the needs of people.

The powers of Satan and evil spirits (demons) likewise will fall before the power of Jesus Christ. Two equal and devastating errors face believers today in regard to Satan and demons. The first error is to deny their existence. The second error is to become overly concerned about them. They exist but cannot stand against the power of Jesus.

TEACHING PLANS

Teaching Plan—Varied Learning Activities

Connect with Life

1. Identify someone in the class or invite someone else you know who is accomplished at fishing. Conduct a brief interview with this fishing expert using questions such as these:
   - How does one learn to become good at fishing?
   - What kind of equipment do you need? What skills do you need?
   - How do you decide where to go fishing?

- If you were "fishing" for people, how would you apply your skills and knowledge?

At the conclusion, thank your fishing expert.

2. Say, *Today we will study Jesus as he called his first disciples and told them they would be fishers of people. Let's evaluate how we would stack up ourselves.*

Guide Bible Study

3. Enlist someone to read Matthew 4:12–17 while the class listens for what Jesus did and what his message was. Receive reports. Lead the class in brainstorming a definition of the term "repent." Then divide the class into small groups (no more than six people each) and instruct each group to create an acrostic for the word REPENT. (In an acrostic, each letter of the word starts another word or phrase.) Call for presentations from each group. As needed, refer to the information about repentance under "Jesus' Message" in the *Study Guide.*

4. Read the section in the *Study Guide* about the kingdom of heaven (final two paragraphs under "Jesus' Deeds"). Tell the class that you are going to have a friendly debate about whether the kingdom of heaven is already in place or has not yet occurred. Divide into two groups, assigning one to take the position that the kingdom of heaven is *already,* and the other to take the position that it is *not yet.* You can make the assignments to each group, or you can allow members to choose which side they want to support. Allow several minutes for the two groups to determine their points, and then have each one present. If you like, you can have one-minute rebuttals from the opposite side. Be sure to keep things light and friendly, not hostile! Conclude by stressing that both sides are correct: Jesus inaugurated the kingdom of heaven, but it will not be fully realized until his return.

5. Form small groups of six or fewer people each. Instruct each group to write a one-act screenplay about Jesus calling the disciples as described in Matthew 4:18–21. The screenplay should include

details about the setting, camera angles, dialogue, and movement of the characters. After several minutes, have each group read or act out their screenplay.

6. Enlist someone to read 4:18–21 aloud while the class considers the cost for Simon Peter, Andrew, James, and John to follow Jesus. Lead the group to brainstorm what the cost might be for us to follow Jesus. After a few minutes, ask, *Are there any costs here that you would not pay to follow Jesus?* Allow silent or voiced response. Then lead members in silent or voiced prayer that they might become bolder and more sacrificial as they follow Jesus.

Encourage Application

7. State that the *Study Guide* (final sentence under "Jesus' Message") says, "Jesus preached a sense of urgency because God was about to do something new and powerful." Lead a discussion with questions such as these:
    *   Why did Jesus want the people to have a sense of urgency about the kingdom of heaven?
    *   Should we have a similar sense of urgency? Do we? Why or why not?
    *   How would you do things differently if you were sure Christ would return one month from today?

8. Lead the class to brainstorm some ways people like us can respond to Jesus and can proclaim the gospel in word and deed. Write the answers on a markerboard. After generating a list, invite the class to privately select one or more items that they will do this coming week.

Teaching Plan—Lecture and Questions

Connect with Life

1. See whether anyone in the class is currently enrolled in an educational course. Ask this person—or the whole class if you like—*What*

does it take to be a good student? Jot the answers on a markerboard. Lead the class to evaluate how many of these qualities they have, and whether they would be a good student. Then say, *Today, we will talk about Jesus and his students, or disciples. As we look at those first followers, let's consider how we measure up as effective students and disciples of Jesus.*

Guide Bible Study

2. Read Matthew 4:13–16. Also read John 1:43–46 and John 7:50–52. Point out that these passages suggest that people discounted Jesus because of where he came from. Ask, *Do we ever discount people because of their hometown or background? Why? Do we have similar expectations about where or how God might reveal himself?*

3. Lead the class to create a definition of the term "repent." Then lead a discussion using questions such as these:
    - How do most people use the word "repent"?
    - What do you think is the biblical definition?
    - In what spheres of life might we "repent" (for example, the *Study Guide* mentions doing a U-turn when we've driven our car past a turnoff).
    - Do Christians need to repent just once? If so, when does that happen? If not, when or how often do we need to repent?

    Refer to the information about repentance under "Jesus' Message" in the *Study Guide.*

4. Read Matthew 4:18–21. Note that James and John appear to have left their father's fishing business without asking questions or requiring promises. Ask, *If it were you, what questions would you have asked, and what promises would you have required?* Allow the group to generate several ideas. Next ask, *How do you think Jesus would have answered these questions from James and John?* Again, take answers. Then continue the discussion with questions like these:
    - If we were talking with Jesus about following him, what questions or promises would we add to the list?
    - How do you think Jesus would answer us?

- Can you think of a time in your life when you did something that, looking back, you might not have done had you known what was in store?

Encourage Application

5. Refer to the questions in the *Study Guide*. Take several minutes and lead the class in self-examination using the questions. Be sure to allow enough time for people to think through their responses.

6. Say, *Christians believe that when we accept Christ, we begin to change and become more like Jesus. If you are already a believer, what are three ways you feel you have changed since you accepted Jesus as your Lord and Savior? If you have not made the decision to accept Christ, what are three ways you wish you might be changed?* Allow several minutes of quiet for this exercise. Conclude with a prayer of thanks that the Holy Spirit brings believers to change and a petition that each person might be even more willing to change to be more Christlike. If you think you have non-believers in your group—and you might be surprised—be sensitive with this activity. Encourage people to trust in Christ.

FOCAL TEXT
Matthew 5:1–12

BACKGROUND
Matthew 5:1–16

MAIN IDEA
Followers of Christ are
blessed in ways that reverse
all ordinary expectations.

QUESTION TO EXPLORE
How is life in God's kingdom
different from ordinary life?

TEACHING AIM
To lead adults to identify
how the Beatitudes provide
encouragement and hope for
living as a follower of Jesus

LESSON SIX
*The Great
Reversal*

UNIT THREE
Hope in Jesus'
Teachings

BIBLE COMMENTS

Understanding the Context

The Gospel of Matthew tells the story of Jesus through a series of narratives interspersed with five extended discourses of his teachings
(Matthew 5—7; 10; 13; 18; 23—25).[1] The Sermon on the Mount is the
first and longest of these discourses. In all likelihood, Jesus originally
gave these teachings in varied forms at many times and places during his
Galilean ministry. They reflect the dominant themes of Jesus' teaching
and life mission.

Preceding the Sermon on the Mount, Matthew recounted the ministry of John the Baptist, the baptism of Jesus, his temptations in the
wilderness, and the beginning of his Galilean ministry (Matt. 3:1—
4:23). Jesus experienced growing success in this stage of his ministry.
He attracted crowds of the curious as well as those hungry to hear an
authentic word from God. He began to call out some people to whom
he would entrust the responsibility of sharing the good news of God's
kingdom in special ways. These disciples needed special training. The
content of the Sermon on the Mount provided the core teachings for
their preparation for ministry.

Many Christians and non-Christians alike regard the Sermon on the
Mount as the heart of Jesus' teachings concerning the nature of the life
of faith. Although the Sermon on the Mount is essential to understand
what it means to follow the way of Jesus, it does not reflect the entire
gospel. The demands of the Sermon are impossible to meet without
the reality of God's saving and empowering grace. The content of these
teachings deals with how a true disciple lives rather than how one can
become a disciple.

The Beatitudes provide a profile of the citizen of God's kingdom.
They describe a person whose priority is to know and do the will of
God in all of life's circumstances. Upon reading them, people today
are apt to say they are too impractical or demanding to be a guide for
life in the real world. The Beatitudes run counter to much of today's
conventional wisdom. They appear to turn the values of an aggressive,
acquisitive, and assertive society upside down. Only those who risk

swimming against the stream of prevailing cultural values discover in the Beatitudes a surprising way to enduring joy.

Interpreting the Scriptures

The Setting of the Sermon (5:1–2)

Jesus went "up the mountain." He may have wanted to get above the crowd in order to address them more effectively. More likely, he was withdrawing from the crowd to concentrate on teaching the disciples who had begun to follow him with more than casual interest.

The term "disciple" refers to a learner. In Jesus' day, a disciple often followed a teacher with the intent of mastering the teacher's thought and becoming equipped to interpret it to others. Early in his ministry, Jesus recognized how important such disciples would be for the future of the gospel and of the kingdom of God.

Matthew noted Jesus sat down before teaching. This was the customary posture taken by a rabbi as he taught.

The Way to Unexpected Joy (5:3–12)

The Beatitudes reflect the character of Christ himself, character that he expected his followers to imitate. In our materialistic society, these words provide a distinctly different view of the meaning of fulfillment in life. Each beatitude contains Jesus' citation of a specific quality of character, which is followed by an affirmation of a result.

5:3. Jesus described people who embody the qualities in verses 3–11 as "blessed." The term, also translated *happy*, expresses a sense of enduring well-being and irrepressible joy. Although "blessed" may be archaic to some today, *happy* may seem too superficial in its popular usage to carry Jesus' full meaning in the Beatitudes. The blessedness of the Christian is not determined by external factors often seen as prerequisites for happiness. It depends on the quality of the relationship between the disciple and the master and the conduct that grows out of that relationship.

The blessed disciple is "poor in spirit." This person recognizes the need for spiritual direction and power. This characteristic is the opposite of human pride and self-sufficiency, which the Bible sees as the source of sin. The rule of God cannot be a reality in lives that have already placed self on the throne. In Luke's account, Jesus referred simply to "you who are poor" (Luke 6:20). In Matthew, it is clear the crucial issue was not whether a person experienced material poverty or wealth. Jesus was concerned about what one's material situation could do to a person's spirit. Physical poverty may make it easier for a person to become humble and open to the reign of God than the possession of wealth.

God will truly and completely reign in the lives of such people ("theirs is the kingdom of heaven"). The beatitude points to a future realization of the full blessings of the kingdom, but also affirms a significant promise for the present. The blessing does not refer to one's possession of the kingdom as much as one's full participation in it.

5:4. Jesus pronounced this beatitude to those who handle sorrow in the same manner in which they approached all of life's experiences. They submitted even their grief to the Lordship of Christ. The mourners are not simply those who feel sorrow for themselves in their own pain and sin. They also feel deeply with others who hurt. They identify compassionately with those who experience pain, death, failure, and injustice.

"They will be comforted" literally means *they shall be made strong.* The promise goes beyond the emotional consolation Christ brings the believer in times of sorrow. The mourner can be fortified by the strengthening presence and wisdom of God.

5:5. In contemporary usage, *meekness* often conveys the idea of weakness or withdrawal. It represents a cowardly response of people who let anyone run over them. In contrast the Bible uses *meekness* as a term of strength. The word carries the concept of self-discipline. The "meek" are people who are in control of themselves because they are controlled by a higher will than their own.

Becoming meek may be compared to the process of breaking a wild horse. The horse is broken not to destroy its strength, but to control it and channel it to the accomplishment of positive purposes. In a similar way, the "meek" are not people whose strength has been dissipated but are people whose power has been enhanced because they have come under the control of God. The "meek" have been gentled by God.

Compare this beatitude to Psalm 37:11. The phrase "inherit the earth" was used in the Old Testament in a literal way to speak of the possession of the Promised Land. In the psalm, however, it appears to be used in a figurative sense to mean *to possess divine blessing.*

In this world, the earth appears to belong to self-assertive, aggressive people. Their actual possession of the earth, however, can be more apparent than real. Psalm 73, in its entirety, provides excellent commentary on this beatitude.

5:6. The true disciple pursues righteousness with the intensity that a hungry and thirsty person desires food and water. The follower of Jesus demonstrates total commitment and urgency to implement God's ways in the world. "Righteousness" can refer to the cause of civic righteousness and social justice or to personal goodness and integrity. Citizens of the kingdom of heaven strive for a life that reflects the character of God in the world. Jesus said those who refuse to be satisfied with anything less than the righteousness of God in their lives will not be disappointed.

5:7. "Mercy" describes God's capacity to forgive sin and show compassion for people, even when they do not deserve it. Mercy expresses itself in concrete and costly acts that make love visible and believable. The distinctive quality of God's mercy is expressed in the Hebrew word *hesed,* used frequently in the Old Testament of God's covenant love for Israel. Translated as *mercy* or *steadfast love, hesed* expresses the tenacious strength of God's love that "endures forever" (Psalm 100:5).

Mercy cannot be paid back; it can only be passed on. This beatitude reflects a consistent theme in the teaching of Jesus. The forgiven are to become forgivers; the blessed become bearers of blessing. This beatitude may appear to mean that the receipt of God's mercy is conditional on one's giving mercy to others. This is similar to the petition in the Lord's Prayer, "Forgive us our debts, as we also have forgiven our debtors" (Matt. 6:12). One who is incapable of showing mercy to others reveals the lack of a full experience of receiving God's transforming grace.

5:8. The "pure in heart" have singleness of mind. "Pure" means *without blemish, mixture, or alloy.* True Christians no longer live with a divided self. In the words of the psalmist, they have the capacity to worship God with "all that is within me" (Psalm 103:1). "Heart" is commonly used in Scripture to refer to more than human emotions. It includes mind and will as well. One's heart is the control center of one's life.

The promise is that this disciple will "see God." The ultimate vision of God lies beyond this life, and yet one who is single-minded in commitment can experience God's presence here and now. As Paul wrote, Christ's followers now "see in a mirror, dimly, but then we will see face to face" (1 Corinthians 13:12). In Christian history, the promise in this Beatitude was related to the idea of the *beatific vision*, the immediate and direct sight of God known only in the glory of heaven.

5:9. Peacemakers take the initiative to bring peace out of conflict. Peace is more than the cessation of conflict or hostility. The peacemaker seeks to bring about relationships of acceptance, understanding, and good will. Jesus commended the one who *makes* peace, not simply the peaceful person or a lover of peace. To be a peacemaker requires courage to take initiative in the middle of alienation and conflict and demonstrate a willingness to pay the cost of a ministry of reconciliation.

"Children of God" refers to the believers' identity with God in character and action. Authentic disciples of Jesus bear unmistakable resemblance to the character of God in their daily lives. Jesus assured the peacemakers they are doing God's kind of work in God's way, and it shows.

5:10–12. The way of the Christian is not easy. In the best of times, true faith experiences tension within its culture. In the worst settings, a person can face open persecution for living according to the way of Jesus.

Jesus referred to suffering caused by a believer's commitment to live as a true representative of Christ in spite of the consequences. In such suffering, Jesus promised the disciples grace to endure and gave reasons to rejoice. One can rejoice when experiencing false accusations and knowing that one is acting in identity with the serving and suffering Christ. One also rejoices because of the promise of future reward. The belief that present injustice and inequity will be compensated in a future time and realm has been a basic part of the Christian theology of hope. One can also take heart because "the prophets who were before you" also suffered for their faithful actions in service of God. Christians can know they are in good company.

The Disciple's Influence (5:13–16)

Jesus used two analogies drawn from common experience to describe the influence of his disciples in the world. His followers were to penetrate the culture, as salt works to preserve food and light dispels darkness to reveal reality. Interpreters have proposed a number of specific uses of salt and light that might be applied to the disciples' mission in the world. Jesus did not explain the specific functions of salt and light he had in mind. Instead, he let these metaphors lodge in the minds of his hearers to continue to unfold their meaning.

Jesus made it clear that his disciples were to be good stewards of the experience they had with him. They were to reflect the grace and truth they had found in him to others. They were to act so that people would see their good works, but not to call attention to themselves. Their influence would point people beyond themselves to the source of their life and light.

Focusing on the Meaning

People today are apt to turn away from the Beatitudes as a model for life, finding them to be too demanding or impractical. Some, however, may have experienced enough failure or achieved enough empty success to open them to consider anew the way of the Beatitudes. People may give new hearing to these ancient words of Jesus because their heart hunger has not been satisfied by this culture's prescriptions for joy. The person who takes these teachings of Jesus seriously can come to some surprising conclusions, including these:

- What we want in life is not necessarily what we need. In a materialistic society, we are conditioned to think of things as necessities which really are luxuries or trivialities. Although these may bring passing pleasure, they are incapable of giving abiding joy.
- While a person on the outside may see the way of Jesus as only a life of sacrifice and subservience, the follower of Jesus experiences it as the way to fulfillment and freedom. The disciple discovers true meaning in giving control of life to the One who created and redeemed it.

- While some search for happiness through escape from the challenges of the real world, the Christian discovers a higher happiness in engaging the problems and pain of the world in the spirit of Christ.
- What we experience in our relationship to God is not to be kept to ourselves but shared. What God has done for us, God desires to do through us for others.
- When the church embodies the qualities described in the Beatitudes, it has power to make a distinctive difference in the world.

As your study group considers all of the Beatitudes, which do they find most difficult to understand? Which is the most challenging to apply to their lives? What are the clearest examples of each of the Beatitudes they have seen demonstrated in the lives of others?

TEACHING PLANS

Teaching Plan—Varied Learning Activities

Connect with Life

1. Food always serves as a great time of fellowship and, in this case, a great illustration of reversal (from hunger to satisfaction!). You might want to plan to have a group breakfast on this morning. Enlist some of the members to bring sweet rolls, sausage and biscuits, ham and biscuits, and donuts. Enlist a second group to bring some fresh fruit, health and energy bars, bagels, and cups of yogurt. Let the members enjoy whatever they want. This offers a great opportunity to invite guests and to bring the group together.

2. After an appropriate length of time, call the group to order and begin the class. Walk over to the breakfast buffet table and talk about the food. Thank everyone who brought the food and share

what good cooks your class is "blessed" to have. Tell everyone that you instructed people on what to bring. Then talk about the *good* versus *good-for-us* food, the *good-tasting* versus the *healthy* food, and even sometimes, the *good-looking* food versus the *heart healthy* food. Assure them that this is a not a lesson about diet, but a lesson on the *great reversal* of the Christian Life, the world's view as opposed to being "blessed."

Guide Bible Study

3. Share with the class that the lesson today is about being "blessed" as a Christian. In advance, enlist someone to summarize the article titled "True Blessing" in the *Study Guide*.

4. Then ask the members to form as many as four groups, with two to six people in each group. In advance, write the names of the Beatitudes with the Scripture reference for the Beatitudes on an index card. Make an index card for each of the Beatitudes. Make sure the Beatitudes index cards are not in the order as they appear in Matthew 5. Give two cards to each of the four groups. (If needed, make adjustments according to the number of people present.) Provide these instructions to the group:

    (1) Study the assigned beatitude(s) to arrive at one or two ideas about what it means.

    (2) Identify actions that demonstrate the beatitude, some way of living out each of their assigned Beatitudes.

    (3) Plan a way to act out your assigned beatitude and see whether the class members can guess it. This is not acting out the beatitude, but rather acting out an action the beatitude would take in real life.

    (A copy of these instructions is available in "Teaching Resource Items" for this study at www.baptistwaypress.org.) After about ten minutes, have each group report.

Encourage Application

5. Refer to the case study in the *Study Guide*. Ask the members to stay in the same small groups they were in for step 4. Instruct them to list five ways Grace Baptist Church could minister to the prisoners and their families. Then ask them to think about five ways they will practice the Beatitudes in their own communities. (A copy of these instructions is available in "Teaching Resource Items" for this study at www.baptistwaypress.org.) Ask further, *How do the Beatitudes provide encouragement and hope for living as a follower of Jesus?*

6. Lead the class to bow their heads for prayer. Use questions 3 and 5 in the *Study Guide* to lead a time of reflection during the closing prayer. Close the prayer with requests for encouragement to members to discover ways to enact the Beatitudes in their lives.

Teaching Plan—Lecture and Questions

Connect with Life

1. Tell the story of Melody from the beginning of the lesson in the *Study Guide*. Emphasize how Melody's church brought blessing to Melody during a time of great challenges in her life. Lead the group to comment on how both the church and Melody received blessings through the experience. Emphasize the reversal that occurred with Melody as she was able to find blessing in her difficult experience.

2. State that today's lesson shows Jesus teaching that "blessed" or *happy* for the Christian can be a great reversal from the ideas of the world.

Guide Bible Study

3. Before the session, make a chart like the following one:

Beatitudes	Meaning	Actions
Poor in spirit		
Mourn		
Meek		
Hunger and thirst		
Merciful		
Pure in Heart		
Peacemaker		
Persecuted		

Use the chart to guide the members to define the meaning of each beatitude. Use ideas in the *Study Guide* and "Bible Comments" in this *Teaching Guide* as needed. After you discuss the Beatitudes in this way, lead members to identify ways each of the Beatitudes can be applied in today's world and in their communities. Jot down ideas under "Actions."

4. Use the questions in the *Study Guide* to guide further discussion of the Beatitudes.

Encourage Application

5. Lead the members to look once again at the chart and reflect on what it means to have these values in today's world. Ask, *In what ways do you think our world would be different if we were more faithful in following the Beatitudes today?* Encourage members to have a **Be**-attitude where they live, work, and play.

6. Close in prayer, asking God to use every person to be a blessing to someone and to be the salt and light for God in the world.

NOTES —————————————————————————————————

1. Unless otherwise indicated, all Scripture quotations in lessons 6–12 are from the New Revised Standard Version.

MAIN IDEA

Followers of Jesus are to pray as Jesus instructed, thus acknowledging their utter dependence on God for all aspects of their lives.

QUESTION TO EXPLORE

How does Jesus' instruction about prayer differ from popular ideas about prayer?

TEACHING AIM

To lead adults to decide to change how they approach prayer in accord with Jesus' instructions

UNIT THREE
Hope in Jesus' Teachings

BIBLE COMMENTS

Understanding the Context

Jesus insisted his disciples' way of life was to be distinctively different from that of the scribes and Pharisees. He left no doubt their standards of conduct should surpass those of Israel's most noted moralists. In Matthew 5:21–48, Jesus gave examples of kingdom righteousness that go far beyond keeping the letter of the law to fulfilling its spirit and intention. One's actions were obviously important, but attitudes and motives were more important. Jesus' shift of focus from actions to motivations continued as he dealt with the difference between the ways his followers and the scribes and Pharisees expressed their religious devotion.

Established religious practices are intended to help an individual grow in a deeper relationship to God and express that relationship more effectively to other people. These basic disciplines in Christianity have developed through centuries, and their roots lie deep in the soil of Judaism. Unfortunately, these practices can also become ways through which a person can express the pride and self-centeredness that distort one's fundamental relationship to God and other human beings. The key to whether a religious practice becomes a blessing or a bane lies in the motivation of the worshiper rather than the ritual correctness of the act.

In Matthew 6:1–18, Jesus addressed the need for right motives in the traditional practices of religion, focusing on giving alms, praying, and fasting. Jesus affirmed the biblical truth that, although human beings are often impressed by outward appearances, God looks upon the heart. Jesus' argument in these verses is not against all public expressions of religion. It is rather a strong indictment of self-serving reasons for acting out one's faith. Here, as in Jesus' previous teaching concerning moral behavior, he stated a general principle and then applied it to specific religious practices.

Interpreting the Scriptures

In the Sermon on the Mount, Jesus contrasted the righteousness of the scribes and Pharisees with his understanding of righteousness by emphasizing the spirit of the law and the motivation for behavior.[1] Jesus warned his disciples against following the way of prayer practiced by many. He also gave them a model for prayer that has been an enduring treasure for Christians through the ages. Jesus' approach was in marked contrast to some of the practices of ritualistic prayer both in Judaism and in pagan worship.

Avoiding Prayer as Performance (6:5–8)

Jesus' primary charge against those who abused the practices of religion was that they had turned them into performances designed to win the attention and applause of others rather than acts of genuine devotion to God. Note Jesus' recurring assessment that their primary motive in almsgiving, prayer, and fasting was to be seen and praised by a human audience. Jesus said that when this happened, they had fulfilled their purpose and received their desired reward. Jesus used their practices as negative examples that missed the meaning of truly religious acts.

6:5. In the time of Jesus, the practice of prayer in Judaism had become highly developed and regimented. People were to pray at stated times and in prescribed language. Jesus appears to suggest that prayer can occur spontaneously at any time ("whenever you pray") and express individual concerns.

The word "hypocrites" often referred to an orator or actor. It came to mean one who pretended to be something one really was not and often carried connotations of insincerity. Jesus described people who used the practices of religion as props as they played their roles in pursuit of human applause.

6:6. Jesus contrasted prayer offered for public consumption with the sincere opening of a believer's heart to God. This verse does not censure all public prayer. There is a vast difference in parading one's piety before others and effectively leading others in prayer. In public prayer within the congregation, one who voices a prayer can help others find their own voice. Such prayer can gather the common concerns of the body and lift them to God in behalf of the people. It can express the praise of the people for shared blessing and the need for guidance as they seek to know and do God's will.

"Your room" can refer to a small storeroom where treasures might be kept. The word may suggest a regular place of prayer filled with spiritual treasures and the memory of experiences with God. The believer is to go to this place that holds vital personal meaning. In this setting, one can commune openly and honestly with God. The phrase "shut the door" conveys the conviction that prayer at its heart is personal and private.

6:7. Just as prayer is not to be understood as a performance to impress the public, neither is it a performance designed to persuade God. Jesus cautioned against babbling empty phrases or meaningless words in prayer. Many believed certain words and phrases were particularly effective in communicating with God. Others evidently thought the length of a prayer determined its effectiveness.

6:8. In prayer one does not provide God with information he does not already know. A person can add nothing to God's understanding of one's circumstances or convince God to care more deeply about one's personal needs. In the confidence God already knows and cares, a disciple prays to discover a new perspective on human concerns, to enlarge one's own understanding rather than God's.

Using a Model for Prayer (6:9–13)

Jesus gave his disciples a way to approach the practice of effective prayer. Although traditionally called *the Lord's Prayer*, Jesus did not offer it for himself but shared it as a model for believers to follow. He did not say, *pray these exact words*, but, "pray then in this way." From the early days of the church, however, the prayer has been used extensively in corporate Christian worship. Matthew's version of the prayer lends itself to liturgical use with its measured cadence and simple words that express the primary concerns of all believers.

A significant feature of the model prayer is its use of personal pronouns in their first-person plural forms. The prayer voices no self-centered concerns, but rather speaks in the language of "our," "us," and "we." This fact in itself guards one against the desire to rush into God's presence with a long agenda of personal concerns and take no thought of their implications for others.

6:9. The disciple's address to God reflects a sense of both intimacy and awe. God is "our Father"—the source of all life and the personal reality who continues to express providential care for all creation. As God's children, we know the Father's name. To know one's name was to know the essence of the person. In biblical culture, the concept of the name of God included God's character and the nature of his redemptive actions within history. At the same time, the name of God was to be "hallowed," held in honor and regarded as holy. Addressing God in prayer acknowledges God's nearness to us but also recognizes God as beyond us and whom we cannot control.

6:10. Jesus' hearers would undoubtedly have heard this petition in light of their expectation of the coming Messiah. It affirms God's sovereignty and anticipates God's decisive action in history. The petition also has a more personal meaning. True prayer begins when one acknowledges dependence on God and accepts the priority of God's will. In this first petition, we do not seek to get what we want from God, but rather to understand God's will and make it our own.

6:11. God is concerned to meet one's needs for survival and sustenance. This petition does not imply people are to pray that God will miraculously supply their needs apart from their own human effort. Neither are they to ask for abundance and wealth. The prayer brings practical concerns for the day before God in the confidence God will meet them. The image of daily bread may have reminded Jewish hearers of God's dependable daily provision of manna and quail for the people of Israel on their journey from Egypt to Canaan (Exodus 16).

Although this petition, "give us this day our daily bread," focuses on one's physical needs, some interpreters in early Christian history spiritualized its meaning. They linked this petition to Jesus' references to his being "the bread of life," his breaking the loaves and feeding the five thousand, and his taking the bread at the Last Supper saying, "This is my body that is for you" (1 Corinthians 11:24). Christian hymnody and devotional literature have perpetuated the idea of the necessity of receiving Christ as daily bread to nurture the spiritual life.

6:12. The root meaning of the term commonly used for forgiveness is *to send away*. To ask for forgiveness is to seek removal of whatever has broken

or distorted our primary life relationships. Forgiveness is essential if resto-
ration of the relationship of people to God and to other human beings is to
occur. Forgiveness is possible because of God's redeeming act in Jesus.

The need for forgiveness comes because human attitudes and actions
have raised barriers people cannot dismantle and created guilt they
cannot remove. In Matthew's version of the model prayer, the need for
forgiveness is said to be "our debts." In verses 14–15, the word used is
"trespasses." Luke used the term "sins" (Luke 11:4).

The experience of God's forgiveness enables the Christian to forgive
others for the things that have separated them. God's forgiveness of us
and our forgiveness of others are closely related in this petition. The
continuation of an unforgiving spirit is evidence that a person has not
fully experienced God's forgiveness. The Christian prays for forgiveness
and the grace to forgive as well.

6:13. The more common translation of "do not bring us to the time of
trial" is "lead us not into temptation" (KJV). The phrase continues the
focus on personal sin and appeals for God's grace and power to help
overcome in the struggles with daily temptation. The translation, "the
time of trial" (NRSV), shifted the focus of the disciples toward the future
time of conflict and struggle many thought would mark the coming of
the kingdom of God and the end of the existing age. Many expected a
time of intensified conflict between the faithful and the forces of "the
evil one." The disciple prays to be spared from this apocalyptic time of
dangerous struggle with Satan.

In older translations, including the King James Version, the prayer
concludes with a doxology that begins "For thine is the kingdom." This
phrase became part of the prayer quite early in Christian worship. It
appears to reflect the influence of the concluding words of prayers
spoken in the Jewish synagogue. The doxology proclaims ultimate power
and glory belong to God alone. Because these words do not appear in the
oldest and best attested Greek texts of Matthew, however, they are omitted from many translations.

Relating Prayer and Practice (6:14–15)

The petition for forgiveness is the only one to which Jesus gave further
explanation. For him, the results of true prayer are not to be measured in

terms of what we receive so much as what we become. Prayer changes us, and our actions toward others are to reflect that change. The experience of being forgiven by God leads a person to forgive others. To become a forgiven forgiver is the goal of the petition. Underlying the petition for forgiveness is the principle that we are not to ask from God what we are unwilling to grant to others. True union with God results in reconciliation with our fellow human beings as well.

Focusing on the Meaning

Finding an effective way to pray is difficult in every age. Ours is no exception. A person can become frustrated by the pervasive cynicism about prayer in a secular culture. One can also be confused by the many approaches that seem to reduce prayer to simple, guaranteed formulas for getting what one wants from God. Believers today who seek to make prayer more meaningful find Jesus' instruction helpful on their spiritual journey. His words can transform the experience of prayer from mere religious ritual into authentic communion with God.

We can learn much by reflecting on Jesus' teaching about prayer in the Sermon on the Mount. Among the life-changing insights we discover in it are these:

- Authentic prayer seeks communion with God as its priority rather than the recognition and approval of those who are impressed by public displays of piety.
- Effective prayer develops in daily discipline. One discovers prayer to be more than words spoken on religious occasions or in times of personal crisis. Prayer becomes a way of life that seeks to know God's presence in every circumstance.
- Helpful prayer determines to be honest with God. Prayer can be characterized in part as pouring out one's heart to God. A person can discover the freedom to say what one really thinks and feels in the presence of one who knows all about us and cares deeply for us. Pretension in prayer only keeps us from expressing the courage to face ourselves as we really are and discovering the person God wants us to become.

- Transforming prayer results in our becoming more like Jesus in our personal relationships. Prayer enables us not only to experience God's grace for ourselves but also to become bearers of grace to others. The test of prayer is not what we get from it but what we become through it.

Sincere prayer demonstrates the reality of hope. In the act of prayer, we express confidence in God's power not only to protect us but also to transform us. We pray to One we believe holds the future. We act on the conviction that God has us and the whole world in his hands.

Teaching Plan—Varied Learning Activities

Connect with Life

1. During the week prior to the class session, collect a number of different kinds of models. (Examples of models: cars, buildings, people. Perhaps a class member has a special interest in this and could be enlisted in advance to bring a collection and report on it briefly.) Pictures of different items can be included in this grouping. At the class session, display the models and pictures you have collected. At the beginning of class, refer to and talk about the different models you have collected. Be sure to refer to the items as *models.*

2. Ask, *What is the purpose of a model?* Somewhere in the discussion, they should conclude that a model is the replica of the real item. Say, *Today we are going to discuss the model prayer that Jesus gave us.*

Guide Bible Study

3. On a table in front of you, place a wallet or purse, clock, and an empty plate. Share comments from these sections of the *Study Guide* lesson: "Be Perfect" and "Proper Practice." Emphasize in the "Proper Practice" section that Jesus' teachings in Matthew 6 about giving, praying, and fasting are not so much about the practices themselves but the proper attitude. Hold up the purse or wallet and say, *It is not about the size or the amount; rather it is about*

surrendering to God's will. Hold up the clock and say, *It is not about the second, minute, or hour; rather it is about creating a priority of prayer.* Hold up the plate and say, *It is not about giving up food; rather it is about focusing on God. It is about our true audience and our attitude toward God. Prayer is communicating with a personal God who loves and cares for us.*

4. Before class, create a worksheet entitled "Praying for His Glory." (A copy is available at www.baptistwaypress.org in "Teaching Resource Items" for this study.) Give members a copy and tell them we are going to develop a pattern to follow in prayer. The worksheet should look like the sample.

PRAYING FOR HIS GLORY
Matthew 6:9–13 (NASB)

(1) "Our Father who is in heaven"—
  • Acknowledge God's relationship to us and God's sovereignty and perfection
  • Submit ourselves to God's power and authority

(2) "Hallowed be Your name"—
  • Recognize God's holiness

(3) "Your kingdom come"—
  • Submit ourselves to God's authority and ultimate rule
  • Pray that God's kingdom will come in its fullness
  • Commit ourselves to actions in line with God's kingdom purposes

(4) "Your will be done, On earth as it is in heaven"—
  • Submit and commit to doing God's will

(5) "Give us this day our daily bread"—
  • Recognize our dependence on God for even our most basic needs

(6) "Forgive us our debts as we also have forgiven our debtors"—
  • Forgive others
  • Ask for God's forgiveness

(7) "Do not lead us into temptation, but deliver us from evil"—
  • Acknowledge your weakness
  • Pray for strength to resist temptation

After you have given out the sheets, suggest that the class pray through the lesson with you. You will talk about each portion of the prayer, using information in the *Study Guide* and "Bible Comments" in this *Teaching Guide*. The group will then pray through that portion. Participants may want to jot down additional thoughts under each item. Enlist people to pray through various portions. Due to the personal nature of portions of the prayer, invite people to pray silently at those points.

5. At the end of the exercise, give the members another "Praying for His Glory" worksheet and encourage them to use it over the next few weeks. Call for progress reports in upcoming class times.

Encourage Application

6. Lead members to get in trios or pairs for a closing time of prayer. Give them time to find a place where they can use the prayer sheet to pray with one or two partners. Encourage them to share specific needs of the class as they pray.

7. As the leader, take time to pray for your members, those who attended, and those who did not attend. Sometime during the week, write a personal note to encourage members to pray as Jesus taught us to pray.

Teaching Plan—Lecture and Questions

Connect with Life

1. As you begin the class, refer to and ask question 1 in the *Study Guide*, "What are some popular misconceptions people have about prayer? How do those ideas affect the way people pray?" Help the class recall public prayers they hear at sports events, rallies, and civic events. Ask, *Are these prayers different from the prayers you hear in church or homes? How?* Write some of the comments on a markerboard or tear sheet so members can see them.

2. Say, *Today we are going to explore Jesus' way of praying as he provided a model for us to use as we pray.*

Guide Bible Study

3. Use the information in the *Study Guide* under the headings, "Be Perfect," "Proper Practice," and "Audience and Attitude" to set the direction of the lesson. Point out that Jesus was emphasizing a proper motivation and attitude for giving, praying, and fasting. Refer to the small article, "Hypocrite," in the *Study Guide* to add emphasis to the "Audience and Attitude" section. Seek to prepare the group to look at prayer in a new light.

4. Ask, *What do you think it means to pray for the glory of God?* Allow the members to discuss the question for a few moments. Then lead them into the *Study Guide* section titled "Praying for His Glory." Stop at each section of the Scripture verses to discuss what the section means when we pray. Add insights as seems helpful from "Bible Comments" in this *Teaching Guide.*

5. Introduce the section, "Praying with Petitions," by asking question 5 in the *Study Guide,* "How do we keep a balance between praying for the needs of the kingdom and praying for our own needs? Which comes more naturally for us?"

6. Lead the group to discuss how praying Jesus' way would affect their prayer lives. Guide the group to discuss how they pray and what is important to them when they pray. Then lead them through the information in "Praying with Petition" in the *Study Guide*, adding insights from "Bible Comments" in this *Teaching Guide* as seems helpful. Be careful to allow discussion to take place on each area of the prayer.

7. After you have discussed the various areas of the model prayer Jesus gave us, ask the Question to Explore, "How does Jesus' instruction about prayer differ from popular ideas about prayer?" Continue by asking, *Why do you think people pray the way they do instead of Jesus' way of praying?* Lead the members to understand that prayer is between them and God and not between them and other people. Prayer is a personal conversation between ourselves and God.

Encourage Application

8. Refer to the small article, "How to Apply this Lesson," in the *Study Guide* Lead the class to consider each item.

9. Call for prayer requests. Ask the group to consider how Jesus would pray for each request. Lead in a time of prayer. As members prepare to leave, encourage them to use this new knowledge as they pray in the coming week.

N O T E S

1. In Luke's Gospel, the setting for the model prayer is the disciples' request for Jesus to teach them how to pray after they had observed him praying (Luke 11:2–4).

MAIN IDEA

Jesus calls us to trust God and focus our lives on God's way rather than on material things.

QUESTION TO EXPLORE

Do we really value God more than we value things?

TEACHING AIM

To lead adults to consider how their lives would be changed if they trusted God and focused their lives on God's way rather than on material things

LESSON EIGHT
Trust, Not Anxiety or Greed

UNIT THREE
Hope in Jesus'
Teachings

BIBLE COMMENTS

Understanding the Context

Jesus' hearers were tempted to place their trust in material things in much the same way people do today. Although most of them had few possessions, they considered wealth to be both a sign of God's blessing and the means to escape their constant worry about survival. They looked for God's Messiah to come to rescue them from their distress and uncertainty. Too often, however, they defined security in the coming kingdom of God in terms of the abundance of things and the reality of overwhelming military and temporal power. Jesus' words in the Sermon on the Mount and throughout his ministry challenged their popular misconceptions.

Economic uncertainty seems to be a fact of life for many people, likely some who will gather for the study of this passage. Retirement savings can erode. Homes can be lost to foreclosure. Crises in trusted financial institutions and unscrupulous lending practices seem to be reported more frequently. In unsettled times, Christian people inevitably ask: Where does our true security lie? What should be our chief concerns in life? Where is the balance between absolute faith in the providence of God and appropriate attention to securing the necessities of life?

The focal passage for today's lesson deals with these fundamental questions and affirms that the rule of God in a person's life can free one from the tyranny of things. Jesus assured his disciples that single-minded trust in God is the key to a life free from anxious care. The passage comes to its climax in verse 33 in the affirmation of one main truth: Giving God absolute priority in life frees one from the fear and uncertainty that comes from placing trust in any lesser reality.

Interpreting the Scriptures

Securing Your Treasure (6:19–21)

6:19. Earthly treasures most likely would have consisted of stores of grain or expensive cloth. In the time of Jesus, much wealth was in the form of fabrics. People took great care to protect such treasures, but they could not absolutely prevent their becoming devalued or destroyed. The moth could take its toll on rugs, hangings, or garments. The word translated "rust" literally means *eating*. Some translate the term as *worm*, possibly referring to destructive vermin or rodents.

The image suggested by "thieves break in" was of a burglar who could simply dig through the mud walls of a house to get to its contents.

Treasure today may be in the forms of stocks, bonds, or certificates of deposit in a bank. It may be in real estate with carefully drawn deeds. Yet, sophisticated instruments of wealth can be threatened by equally sophisticated means of thievery. Ours is the day of identity theft, computer hackers, forged documents, and other means of gaining what rightfully belongs to another. Earthly treasures in any age provide no absolute assurance of permanent security.

6:20. The Jews of Jesus' day were familiar with the concept of heavenly treasure. References in rabbinical literature indicate heavenly treasure consisted of deeds of kindness that one did on behalf of others. It was also seen as the character a person developed through the study of the law and through doing good works.

Jesus clearly taught heavenly treasures were the result of taking the will of God as life's highest priority and reflecting that commitment consistently in daily life. One who is rich in heavenly treasure lives with self-giving love toward others. In relation to material things, the person who is truly rich lives with a sense of stewardship before God of all one has. The guiding question of such a life is not: *How can I increase and preserve everything I can for myself?* but rather: *How can I use what I have to enhance the kingdom of God and help others discover its value?*

6:21. Jesus' words may have reflected a commonly accepted proverb in the culture. When a person has invested in something, one's continuing and often consuming interest is sure to follow. The reverse of the proverb is also true; for when we believe passionately in a cause, we will likely give of our resources to support it. Jesus was obviously concerned that we give of ourselves and our substance to realities that endure. Note Jesus' story of the rich fool in Luke 12:13–21 as a graphic illustration of Jesus' warning.

Avoiding the Disaster of Divided Loyalty (6:22–24)

Jesus followed his appeal for single-minded obedience to the will of God with two illustrations warning his disciples of the danger of attempting to live with divided loyalties. He reminded them of the serious consequences when the body has a diseased eye or when a slave attempts to serve two masters. Each illustration applies to the potential peril of material possessions.

6:22–23. Jesus compared the function of the healthy eye in the body to that of a lamp in a small, one-room Palestinian house. The healthy eye, the single or sound eye, was the means by which the body could experience light and objects in the world outside itself. Some have compared the eye to a window that conveys light into a room. When the eye is healthy, the entire body is able to experience a clear understanding of the objects that come into its view. Just as the eye illuminates the physical body, there is a kind of spiritual eye, a human capacity to perceive spiritual reality. If this capacity is divided or distorted, a person remains in spiritual darkness.

6:24. Jesus emphasized the same basic truth through the use of an illustration taken from the realm of slavery. In the ancient world, sharing ownership of slaves appears to have been legal. Jesus saw this arrangement of serving "two masters" as unsatisfactory. Masters would inevitably make competing demands for the slave's service. The slave would respond favorably to one and reject the other.

"God and wealth" are compared to the two masters who claim the loyalty and service of the slave. The word translated "wealth" or "mammon" (KJV) may refer to something stored up or something that has become the object of one's trust. It may simply refer to property and carry no negative connotation. In Jesus' usage here, however, "wealth" stands as a personification of material things that demand the kind of trust that produces a false sense of security.

Escaping the Folly of Anxious Care (6:25–32)

This section is the most poetic one in the Sermon on the Mount. Jesus' use of figures of speech from nature reveals his keen observation of the natural order. Jesus made his points strongly, stating them in radical ways without qualifications.

6:25. One older translation of the phrase "do not worry," "take no thought" (KJV), may leave the impression that Jesus counseled against planning for the future or having appropriate concern for one's physical needs. However, Jesus' intention was to warn the disciples against *pre-occupation* with material things. He was concerned that their excessive concern about the means for living could distract them from discovering the meaning of life.

Most of the people to whom Jesus and the disciples ministered were not the rich who were anxious over their possession of life's luxuries. Rather, they were the poor who struggled continuously to make ends meet. Rich and poor alike can become preoccupied with the pursuit and preservation of material things. Both need the reminder that what seems at times to be most urgent may not be most important. Jesus' rhetorical questions served to focus attention on life's true priorities.

6:26. Jesus did not counsel idleness. The birds were not idle; they simply did not concern themselves with things beyond their control. Jesus instructed the disciples to take note of God's care of creation and to rest assured in God's care for them as well. He called them to be free from anxiety over things they could not control.

6:27. Interpreters offer two basic interpretations of this verse. One focuses on the impossibility of increasing a person's physical height by making sustained effort to do so. The other focuses on worry about extending the time of one's life. Jesus pointed to the impossibility of extending one's life through worry. Anxiety works to shorten rather than lengthen life. Stress-induced illness takes a frightening toll in our contemporary culture.

6:28–29. The word used for "lilies" applied to all kinds of wild flowers. Many scholars believe that the specific reference may be to the anemone, whose scarlet color would lend itself to the comparison with the royal robes of King Solomon. Jesus emphasized that flowers simply grow according to their nature and do not concern themselves with what is beyond their control. God clothes them in unmatched splendor, and this is a clue that God will do the same for people.

6:30. The ovens commonly used for baking in a Palestinian home burned dried grass and other matter for fuel. Jesus used this image to contrast the brief existence of the beautiful but perishable flowers with the greater worth of human beings. Human life is of greater value than the flowers of the field. Like flowers, human existence also comes to an end, but people can have an assurance of God's constant care in this life and hope for eternity.

Throughout his ministry Jesus reminded his followers that excessive fear and worry were a result of their limited ("little") faith. For him, nature held daily reminders of the providential care of God for all of creation, especially for people.

6:31–32. As in verse 25, Jesus urged his hearers not to "worry." The word can refer to becoming distracted and distraught. Jesus called them to refocus their attention on life's main purpose and enduring values. Understanding "Gentiles" to mean *heathen* provides a clearer reference to any person who seeks to focus on material things and live without reference to the priority of God's rule. In contrast to the Gentiles, a disciple lives with the confidence that the "heavenly Father knows" one's needs. Jesus affirmed this also in his instructions concerning prayer (Matthew 6:8). Disciples do not have to pray to inform God of their needs. Neither do they have to work and worry as if securing the necessities of life depended on their efforts alone.

Embracing the Priority of God's Kingdom (6:33–34)

6:33. This challenge of Jesus is a key verse in the Sermon on the Mount. The follower of Jesus is to give absolute priority to the rule of God in his or her life. Jesus stated the demand and the promise given to the kingdom citizen in unconditional terms.

The phrase, "strive first for the kingdom," means to embrace the rule of God as life's highest priority. This is the antidote to the misplaced treasure, the blurred vision, the divided loyalty, and the anxious care about things that distort the meaning of life. The terms "kingdom" and "righteousness" emphasize the reign of God within a person and the quality of life that flows from that relationship. In relation to things, kingdom righteousness expresses a capacity for absolute trust in God to provide for the material needs of life.

The promise of being given "all these things" must be interpreted in light of the preceding verses. They reflect concern for the basic necessities of life more than a desire for its luxuries. The promise affirms that the person in whom God rules supremely will have the necessities of life and all that one needs to fulfill one's ministry as a Christian disciple.

6:34. Jesus challenged his followers to learn to live one day at a time. He concluded with what may have been a traditional proverb. Since each day brings its own cares, it is foolish to borrow tomorrow's trouble today. Giving priority to God in all things frees the disciple to make the most of each day without worrying about problems in the future.

Focusing on the Meaning

The basic presuppositions of this passage are quite different from those that dominate twenty-first century materialistic American culture. American culture places ultimate value on the possession of things and celebrates the human capacities necessary to acquire them. Yet, the outcome of such faith in things fails to produce enduring fulfillment and well-being. Jesus focused on the quality of one's relationship to God as the ultimate key to experiencing life with meaning and joy. Jesus' teaching provides a timely reminder about life's true values and the way to experience them.

We may pursue the acquisition of material things at too high a cost. We may gain the world but in the process lose our own souls. We may reach our goals but discover they fail to satisfy our deepest needs.

We may attempt to live with divided commitments to God and material things, only to realize that such splintered loyalties make an integrated life impossible. Jesus calls us to single-minded commitment to God alone.

We may be assured that God knows our needs and is concerned that they be met. Belief in God's providence is more than merely a theological statement for the Christian. It is the confident trust in God's power to meet our daily needs. This trust does not release us from the responsibility for planning and working to provide for life's necessities. It frees us, however, from the anxious care that the total effort depends on us alone.

We are to put the greatest importance in life on seeking to know and do the will of God. Making the rule of God in our lives the first priority brings the rest of life into its proper perspective. In serving God, we come to know the relative value of things in life and come to respond to the things we receive with an attitude of profound gratitude to God.

TEACHING PLANS

Teaching Plan—Varied Learning Activities

Connect with Life

1. In advance of the class session, find or make a container that resembles a treasure chest. Place on the outside of the chest the words "Life Treasures." Prepare a set of index cards or sheets of paper with the following words: *faith, comfort, hope, confidence, expectation, dependence, relevance, conviction, belief, worry, fear, nervousness, concern, uneasy, apprehension, disquiet, fretfulness, selfishness, hoard, gluttony, voracious, covetous, insatiable, hunger, self-indulgent, greedy.* (A copy of these words can be downloaded from "Teaching Resource Items" for this study at www.baptistwaypress.org.) Put one word on one card for twenty-six cards. Place the cards inside the treasure chest and take it to class.

2. Begin the lesson by talking about the treasures of life. Show the members the chest and ask them what they would put in their treasure chest of life. Take a few responses, and then ask the members to take cards until all of them are gone. Start going around the room and ask members to look at the word, tell the class what the word is, and let the class decide whether the word is one of the true, godly treasures of life. Ask the member to explain why he or she thinks the word represents a treasure of life or not. Explore whether the world sees the word as a treasure. After reading all

the cards and putting them in the chest or rejecting them, tell the class that the lesson today is on the treasures of life according to God's view.

Guide Bible Study

3. Say, *It is important we store up the right kind of treasure and put it in the right place.* Invite someone to read Matthew 6:19–21 while the class listens for what the passage says about storing treasure. Ask, *How have you found these verses true in your experience?* Use the information in the *Study Guide* under "Storing the Right Treasure" and in "Bible Comments" in this *Teaching Guide* to explain and apply the verses. After discussing the section, ask the class to suggest what they think of when they hear the words "treasures in heaven." Bring an additional supply of index cards and markers so members can write these treasures on the cards, one treasure per card, and put them in the chest. (Treasures might be people, mission efforts, and all things valuable to God.). Lead the class to explain why they feel God sees these particular items as treasures.

4. Enlist someone to read verses 22–24 while the class listens for the two images. Receive responses (eyesight and trying to serve two masters). Call for comments on what they think the images mean. Refer as needed to information in the *Study Guide* under "Having the Right Outlook" and in "Bible Comments" in this *Teaching Guide*. Divide the class into halves. Ask half the class to turn to one or two people next to them and discuss how they think we would view our "treasures" if we saw life more clearly. Ask the other half to discuss with one or two people how they think we would use our money and possessions if we sought to serve God fully.

5. Call for someone to ready verses 25–32 as the group listens for various things mentioned that people worry about. Receive reports. Then use these questions to guide further discussion: *What are some things we worry about? How do we overcome the worry and greed of life? Why do we worry about these things in life if God knows our needs? What did Jesus say we should do instead of worrying?* As you lead a discussion of the last question, introduce and read Matthew 6:33. Ask, *How does that verse speak to you?*

Encourage Application

6. Refer to "Case Study" in the *Study Guide.* Invite discussion of what the couple needs to do in light of this Scripture passage.

7. Invite someone to read the Main Idea from the *Study Guide.* Ask, *What are some ways you have found to put that truth into practice? If we did that, what are some ways in which you think our lives would be different?*

8. Close with a prayer to commit our lives to be kingdom citizens who trust God with everything.

Teaching Plan—Lecture and Questions

Connect with Life

1. Display or otherwise call attention to question 2 from the *Study Guide.* You may want to divide the responses into three categories: money; energy; and time. Enlist someone to write the responses on a whiteboard, chalkboard, or tear sheet.

2. Continue by asking, *How do you set priorities for these areas of life?* Give a few minutes for discussion on how priorities are set in the various areas. Say, *Today's lesson asks us to consider where these things fit into our lives, especially how our lives would be changed if we trusted God and focused our lives more on God's way regarding our possessions.*

Guide Bible Study

3. Read Matthew 6:19–21 while the class listens for the right type of treasure and where this treasure should be stored. Explain the verses by using information in the *Study Guide* and in "Bible Comments" in this *Teaching Guide.* Help members come to grips with the temporal nature of the world's treasure and the eternal nature of heavenly treasures.

4. Ask, *How should we view our possessions from God's perspective?* Let members talk about how God views our material things. After a few minutes, read Matthew 6:22–24. Use information on these verses in the *Study Guide* and in "Bible Comments" in this *Teaching Guide*.

5. Refer to and ask question 3 in the *Study Guide*. After a time of discussion, read Matthew 6:25–34. Focus on what it means to seek the kingdom of God and not the kingdom of the world. Point out that God knows and supplies our needs, as we let him.

Encourage Application

6. Lead the class through the items in "Jesus on Money" in the *Study Guide* to help participants deal with God's view of wealth. Invite comments on each item that contrasts the world's view and God's view.

7. Use questions 4 and 5 in the *Study Guide* to assist the group in making the Scripture passage personal.

8. Say, *Suppose an acquaintance who seems to have many possessions begins a conversation with you tomorrow about how concerned he or she is about finances. If you had opportunity to talk with the person about the ideas in this Scripture passage, what are some things that might be helpful?* After a time of discussion, follow up with this question: *What does this passage say to you yourself about trusting fully in God and focusing your life on God's way rather than on materials things?*

9. Close with a prayer of commitment to live a life that trusts God with everything and with every part of life and not a life filled with anxiety and greed.

MAIN IDEA

Even though all will not
respond to Jesus' message,
the reality that many will
respond means we must
continue to share it.

QUESTION TO EXPLORE

What's the point of sharing
Jesus' message when so
many don't respond?

TEACHING AIM

To lead adults to identify
what the parable of the
sower and the soils means
for their lives, their church,
and the mission of Jesus

LESSON NINE
*Realistic
Encouragement*

UNIT THREE
Hope in Jesus'
Teachings

BIBLE COMMENTS

Understanding the Context

As a pastor, I discovered as I greeted people who were leaving worship how the same sermon could affect people in quite different ways. Many would leave the church each week registering abundant apathy in their lifeless handshakes and mumbled greetings. The comments of others indicated they had heard something quite different from what I had intended to communicate in the message. Some would take offense at something that had been said. Others revealed through their eyes and voices that they had experienced a sacred meeting with God that day. People in the same environment, exposed to the same teaching, can respond in radically different ways. Every teacher or pastor has a weekly reminder of the truth of Jesus' parable of the sower.

Matthew's account of Jesus' ministry and mission in Galilee has alternated narrative and discourse material between the Sermon on the Mount and this study passage. Following the Sermon on the Mount in Matthew 5—7, Matthew focused on Jesus' compassion for people and the way he acted in power to meet their needs. Matthew 8:1—9:38 records nine varied miracles of Jesus consisting of healings, calming a storm, and casting out demons. Note Matthew's summary of this time of teaching, preaching, and healing (Matthew 9:35–38).

During this period, Jesus increasingly focused on mission. He named the twelve disciples who would have major responsibility in the spread of God's kingdom. He prepared them to go out, reminding them of the specific problems they would face, but also assuring them of the resources they would have to accomplish their mission. The second major discourse in Matthew is Jesus' teaching on mission (Matt. 10:1–42).

Jesus continued to attract large crowds and impress the people through his words and deeds. Clearly, however, there was growing opposition to his ministry. Some, including John the Baptist, began to wonder whether Jesus was the Messiah they had expected. The opposition of the religious leaders began to harden. Their hostile exchanges with Jesus became sharper, and controversies over his breaking the Sabbath laws intensified. People were obviously responding to Jesus' words and deeds in radically different ways. In this context, Matthew recorded teachings in the form of parables about people's varied responses to the kingdom of heaven (13:1–42).

Interpreting the Scriptures

Teaching Through Parables (13:1–3a)

13:1–2. The increasingly bitter opposition to Jesus did not deter the multitudes from following him. Many of these people came out of simple curiosity, and their interest would later prove to be superficial. The scene of Jesus' speaking from a boat to the multitudes who lined the shore illustrates his popularity during this period. This teaching was addressed to the crowd rather than to the smaller group of disciples.

13:3a. This first reference in Matthew to Jesus' teaching in parables introduces a series of seven parables. These describe the nature of the kingdom of heaven and the varied response people made to it. This chapter also provides the reasons Jesus used parables as a method of teaching (13:10–17, 34–35, 51–52).

"Parable" literally means something *cast alongside*. A parable conveys a spiritual truth or abstract idea by relating it to a concrete picture drawn from ordinary life. Jesus was a master at employing something familiar in nature or common human experience to communicate new or difficult truths in the realm of the spirit. His parables could be grasped by a child and yet pondered profitably by the most profound adult mind.

A parable can be retained easily in the mind. It can stimulate further thought and more apt applications the longer one reflects on it. A classic definition states that "a parable is a metaphor or simile drawn from nature or common life, arresting the hearer by its vividness or strangeness, and leaving the mind in sufficient doubt about its precise application to tease it into active thought."[1]

A general principle of interpreting parables encourages the reader to discover their primary truth or point of comparison. Their specific details normally do not contain elaborate symbolic meanings, but serve to enhance the central truth. One is to avoid allegorical or fanciful interpretations of details that come from the fertile imagination of the interpreter rather than the substance of the text. Note though that Jesus explained two of the parables—the soils and the tares—in ways that go beyond this basic principle of interpretation.

The Sower, the Seed, and the Soils (13:3b–9)

13:3b. Jesus drew many of his parables from the agrarian life of his hearers. People who first heard this familiar parable knew well the process of working the soil and planting crops. The sight of a man broadcasting seed in a field would have been common.

13:4. The interpreter may naturally ask why the sower would have cast valuable seed in so many undesirable places. The question may be partially answered by understanding what many consider the practice in that day of sowing the seed before the ground was plowed. The ground was tilled later, and some of the seed would inevitably be lost because of the birds or unanticipated soil conditions. (Some scholars do not agree this was the prevailing practice.)

The "path" likely refers to footpaths made through the fields by packing down the plowed earth. Seed that fell there would be vulnerable to hungry birds or winds. Even if the seed were not taken away, it could not sprout on the hard and dry surface.

13:5–6. "Rocky ground" refers to a thin layer of soil that covered a stratum of rock. The excessive heat reflected from the rock below and the direct rays of the sun could cause the seed to sprout quickly. The thinness of the soil would cause tender plants to wither quickly also. The thin soil was unable to hold adequate moisture, and the roots of the young plants would not be able to penetrate the rock to reach any moisture at greater depth.

13:7. In this soil, weed seeds and roots of thorns were already present when the sower went out to sow. These grew faster than the plants from the good seed and choked them out.

13:8. In contrast to the other types, the "good soil" was soft, deep, and clean. It was capable of retaining sufficient moisture to generate the seed and sustain the growing plant until it produced the harvest. The harvest produced in the good soil varied in quantity, but it was abundant.

13:9. Jesus used the common expression of the psalmists and prophets, "let anyone with ears listen," to challenge his audience to hear his words with understanding. Listening was an active and not merely passive experience. Understanding the parable demanded serious thought and reflection, which many would not do. Jesus also implied one could not fully understand his words without being willing to act on them. He called the people to hear and heed, to listen and be willing to act in response.

A Response to Questioning Disciples (13:10–17)

Jesus apparently followed the practice of what today would be called teaching by action and reflection. Following times of public discourse and ministry, he would engage in dialog with his disciples as they sought to understand what they had just seen and heard. In these sessions, Jesus would help the disciples grasp deeper meanings of his teachings and their implications for the disciples' own future ministry.

13:10. The disciples may have wondered why Jesus did not simply spell out his meaning clearly and directly in propositions rather than convey what he meant through stories and figures of speech. One can imagine that the disciples had engaged in conversation among themselves to answer the question: *What did he mean by that?* Such conversations would have demonstrated the power of simple story to engage and challenge the mind.

13:11–12. Jesus acknowledged the difference between his disciples' understanding of the mystery of the kingdom and that of the crowds. The issue in interpreting Jesus' response lies in knowing why this difference existed. Some see in the passage a kind of determinism in which God chose to disclose understanding to one group and deny it to another. Those who take this view see Jesus' purpose in using parables as his intention to confuse rather than enlighten the crowd.

In reality the people themselves, not God, were responsible for their lack of understanding. They had closed their eyes and hardened their hearts to God. They stood in a long line of people who had rejected God's prophets and distorted God's promise of Messiah. They had accepted an understanding of God and a vision of the future that made them incapable of responding to the truth that came in Jesus.

God provided revelation to all who would be open to it and respond to it in faith. People who had demonstrated their capacity to receive God's revelation became able to understand even more. Those who had closed their minds to God's revelation were unable to receive further disclosure of God's grace and instead lived in greater darkness.

13:13. The understanding of this difficult verse will depend on how one interprets Jesus' intention in teaching in parables. Did Jesus tell them to confirm the people in their spiritual darkness? Did Jesus teach in parables as an attempt to reach them in their present condition? The primary thrust of Jesus' life and ministry was his attempt to reach all those who needed to understand God's coming kingdom. The parables were an effective means to open closed minds and hardened hearts.

13:14–15. These verses, quoted from Isaiah 6:9–10, are part of the prophet's vision of God in the temple and his call to go as a prophet to his people. They reflect the disturbing reality that the people who needed God's message of hope would not hear it with understanding or respond to it positively. These verses, as quoted from the Septuagint, a Greek version of the Old Testament, point toward the people's responsibility for shutting their eyes and closing their ears to the prophet's message.

13:16–17. These words express another beatitude, commending the disciples for their openness to God's truth and their willingness to follow it. Because the disciples had the privilege to be part of God's decisive movement of redemption in Jesus, they were able to witness the revelation of God in greater ways than the prophets and others.

Interpreting the Parable of the Sower (13:18–23)

13:18. Jesus provided extensive commentary on the meaning of the parable of the sower. This is an exception to his usual practice as recorded in the Gospels. Usually Jesus let a parable stand on its own to evoke thought and dialog.

13:19. Jesus compared the different soils to people who make varied responses to the word of the kingdom. The focus of Jesus' specific interpretation is on the soils rather than the sower or the seed. He identified one who does not understand the word and soon forgets it with the hard path from which the seed is soon taken away. Note that Jesus interpreted the birds that take away the seed as the "evil one" who snatches the word from the mind.

13:20–21. The rocky soil points to the rootless believer, whose early enthusiasm for the kingdom soon dissipates when difficulties come and inner resources are not present. From the beginning, this has been a typical but troubling response of people to the gospel.

13:22. According to Jesus, the choking thorns of the parable signify "the cares of the world and the lure of wealth." These distractions and entanglements prevent the person from coming to productive maturity in the faith.

13:23. The seed in the good soil represents the believer whose response to the gospel begins well and continues until productive maturity. Inner resources are accessible to this one who endures whatever trial comes. This person is the model for all who hear the word with understanding and respond in enduring faith.

Focusing on the Meaning

In our rapidly changing world, some things remain constant. Among these are the basic spiritual needs of humanity and the enduring power of the gospel of grace. Human responses to the gospel today reflect patterns that prevailed in Jesus' day. Even in our high tech times, we can still gain valuable insight from a parable coming from an ancient agrarian past.

1. The experience of nature and the events of ordinary life can convey eternal spiritual truths. Theologians refer to this as a sacramental universe, meaning that anything in creation can become means through which we know God. Jesus was aware of the potential of even simple things to become vehicles of God's revelation.

2. The response of people to God's revelation in every age is always varied. Regardless of the clarity of the message, some people continue to reject the claims of Christ in their lives. The kinds of soil Jesus cited in the parable are present today just as they were in the first-century culture.

3. Entrance into the kingdom of God involves a person in a process of growth toward productive maturity. Salvation has a beginning point when an individual responds in faith to the good news of Jesus Christ. This decision involves one in a lifelong process of faith seeking understanding and expression.

4. The message of the gospel has the power to produce fruit in the person who is receptive to it. Sower, seed, and soil are each necessary for a successful harvest. The believer works to provide the appropriate setting for the seed's growth, but ultimately God through the seed of the gospel gives the increase.

5. The power of the parable can encourage people to reflect on the quality of their own experience of faith. Through the story a reflective Christian comes to ask a searching question: *What kind of soil am I?*

6. In response to the parable, the contemporary Christian also asks: *What kind of sower am I?* A person who is conscientious about sharing faith with others knows in spite of disappointment in the process that the seed of the gospel can produce good harvest. In this confidence, Christ's followers continue to sow the seed, cultivate the soil, and wait for God to give the increase.

TEACHING PLANS

Teaching Plan—Varied Learning Activities

Connect with Life

1. Enlist four people to role-play a situation at the beginning of the class. Have them come into the room, one by one, after the session has officially started. Greet each of them warmly, in the same manner. Each should respond differently. One is to ignore you, with a blank expression, and leave. The second is to nod or wave at you, but with little response beyond that, and then leave. The third is to greet you warmly and then say abruptly, "Gotta go" or "I'm outta here," and leave immediately. The fourth person is to respond to your greeting by hugging you warmly and standing by your side.

2. After all of the role-plays, explain to the class that this was a role-play about responsiveness. Then signal the three who had left the room to return. Thank all four for their help. Then ask the group to identify the four different types of responses you received (none; some, but very little; mixed; warm acceptance). Ask, *What do you think this has to with our Bible study today?* Say, *Today our lesson is on the parable of the sower and how we are to present the gospel, even though the responses will vary, but knowing that some will respond.*

Guide Bible Study

3. Write or display the heading "Ministry in the Face of Growing Opposition (13:1–3)" from the *Study Guide*. Refer to and summarize the first paragraph in that section in the *Study Guide*. Then hold up a *STOP* sign. (You could make a sign out of red paper or simply write the word STOP on a piece of paper.) Ask, *What are the STOP signs of ministry we face in today's world?* Lead the group to explore personal, cultural, and societal *stop* signs people give to the gospel. Ask, *How do these negative responses make you feel? Do*

they frustrate you, or do they make you ask yourself what the use is in sharing the gospel with people?

4. Ask the group what they think of when they hear the word *parable*. Inquire further, *What is a parable?* Refer the group to paragraph three under "Ministry in the Face of Growing Opposition (13:1–3)" in the *Study Guide*. Add other thoughts from the comments on 13:3a in "Bible Comments" in this *Teaching Guide*.

5. Prepare the class to read Matthew 13:3–9. Form the class into thirds (no movement of people or chairs is needed). Assign one group to think about the sower, the next group to consider the soils, and the last group the seed. Ask the groups to consider their assigned roles in the harvest. Then read Matthew 13:3–9 as each third of the class listens from its assigned perspective. People within the groups can consult with each other, but the whole group does not need to come up with a report. After a few moments, call for several volunteers from each third to report. Each group should have a unique perspective on their roles in the harvest. (Here are some examples: The sower is to sow the seeds so there will be the possibility of a harvest. The soil is to provide an environment for the seed. The seeds are simply to sprout and grow.) Ask, *Which of these elements—sower, soils, seed—is unnecessary?* Emphasize that every part of the process is important.

6. Enlist someone to read Matthew 13:10–17 while the class listens for Jesus' explanation of why he taught in parables. Invite reports. Explain further by using information in "Why Parables (13:10–17)" in the *Study Guide* and "Bible Comments" in this *Teaching Guide*. Emphasize that people choose how to respond to God's message and that response affects how receptive they are to the message in the future. Some people hear and respond, and some refuse to respond, hardening their hearts. Refer to and read or summarize the last paragraph in "Why Parables" in the *Study Guide*.

7. Write on a markerboard or a tear sheet the following outline. Enlist someone to read Matthew 13:18–23. Then summarize the four responses.
   - The Path—Matthew 13:18–19
   - The Rocky Soil—Matthew 13:20–21

- The Thorny Soil—Matthew 13:22
- The Good Soil—Matthew 13:23

Ask the members to read the passage again to themselves and think about the people they see in life who seem to fit into these categories of the parable. Ask, *How do you feel when people respond in these ways?* Remind them that the sower simply spread the seed, knowing that some would sprout and grow even though others would not.

Encourage Application

8. Invite someone to read or summarize "Case Study" in the *Study Guide*. Ask, *How can you encourage your friend?* Let the members discuss ways to encourage the children's worker. Then ask them to seek out someone, perhaps in the early childhood, children, or youth area in your church, the next week to encourage them.

9. Use again the pattern in step 5 of making assignments to thirds of the class. Ask a third of the class to suggest how this parable speaks to them personally. Ask another third to suggest how this parable speaks to their church. Ask the last third to suggest how this parable speaks to the mission of Jesus as a whole. Receive responses.

10. Give everyone in the class a seed. (You could use popcorn kernels for the seeds.) Ask the class to hold the seeds in their hands. Close with a prayer to be faithful sowers of the gospel.

Teaching Plan—Lecture and Questions

Connect with Life

1. As you begin the class, ask, *How do you think the gospel of Jesus Christ is being received in our world today? Why do you think more people are not receptive to the gospel?* Let the class discuss the two questions. Jot the answers on a markerboard or tear sheet.

2. Ask, *How do you think missionaries and other ministers feel when they share the gospel and no one responds?* After a few minutes of discussion, tell the story from the *Study Guide* about the wife in Seattle. Then say, *Those are encouraging words about sharing the gospel. Let us look to see what the Scriptures for today tell us about this subject.*

Guide Bible Study

3. Read Matthew 13:1–3. Share with the class the information from the *Study Guide* section, "Ministry in the Face of Growing Opposition (13:1–3)." Then tell the story about "William Carey: 'Expect Great Things . . . Attempt Great Things'" in the *Study Guide*. Ask, *Why do you think people do not respond to the gospel?* Write responses on a markerboard or tear sheet.

4. Read the parable in Matthew 13:3–9. Give a brief explanation of the different types of soils. Help the group see that the sower was faithful to spread the seeds regardless of the soil conditions.

5. Read Matthew 13:10–17. Explain these verses by using the information in "Why Parables (13:10–17)" in the *Study Guide* and "Bible Comments" in this *Teaching Guide*. Refer to the story of the young woman in the *Study Guide* section to illustrate the depth of commitment needed to know God. Read Jeremiah 29:13, and emphasize that people are to seek God with their hearts.

6. Refer again to the responses in step 3 about why people are not receptive to the gospel in today's world. Encourage the group to consider these responses as you read Matthew 13:18–23. Lead the members to identify types of people that fit into "The Path" (Matt. 13:18–19); "The Rocky Soil" (13:20–21); "The Thorny Soil"(13:22); and "The Good Soil" (13:23). At the end of this section, ask, *What was the response of the sower to the different types of soil?* Note that it was the same; the sower simply kept sowing the seeds.

7. Use the questions from the *Study Guide* to bring further understanding and application.

Encourage Application

8. Continue the discussion by asking, *What meaning for your life does this parable suggest to you?* Follow with, *What meaning do you think this parable might have for our church?* Before class, collect some pictures of people in different life situations, pictures that represent homeless people, business people, families, children, and youth. Ask the group to think about people with whom they have contact within these categories. Lead them to think further about how receptive they are to the gospel. Ask whether they themselves are sowing seeds of the gospel in their lives.

9. Give each member a nail. Share that the plow Jesus used to break up the ground of a hard heart was the nail that proved his love for every person. Ask them to hold the nail as you close with a prayer to be faithful sowers of the gospel of Jesus Christ.

NOTES

1. C H. Dodd, *The Parables of the Kingdom*, rev. ed. (Charles Scribner's Sons, 1961), 5.

FOCAL TEXT
Matthew 17:1–13

BACKGROUND
Matthew 16:13—17:13

MAIN IDEA
In Jesus' transfiguration
experience, God confirmed
again that he was well pleased
with Jesus, who would be
crucified and then resurrected.

QUESTION TO EXPLORE
What does God's
affirmation of Jesus' costly,
selfless ministry mean
for how we are to live?

TEACHING AIM
To lead adults to state what
God's affirmation of Jesus in
the transfiguration experience
means for how they are to live

LESSON TEN
Affirmation of the Way of the Cross

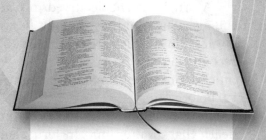

UNIT FOUR
Hope in Jesus' Glorification

BIBLE COMMENTS

Understanding the Context

Jesus' public ministry in Galilee met with growing success. Crowds in great numbers gathered to hear Jesus, and his reputation spread throughout the region. As Jesus continued to minister through preaching, teaching, and healing, many became profoundly impressed. Religious leaders, however, were threatened by his growing popularity. They could not deny Jesus' mighty acts of compassionate healing, and neither could they effectively respond to his fresh interpretations of Israel's faith. His words reached the hungry hearts of the people with an authenticity they could not match with their recitals of elaborate oral tradition.

Jesus' works and words, however, evoked increasing questions and led people to reach opposite conclusions about him. Some were hostile questions designed by opponents to discredit him. Some were the searching questions of people who wanted to understand the implications of his proclamation of the kingdom of God for their lives. What Jesus did and said inevitably caused people to ask who he really was.

Jesus' rejection in his hometown of Nazareth (Matthew 13:54–58) marks the beginning of a transition in Matthew's Gospel from a public ministry toward an increasing focus on training the Twelve. Although his public ministry continued, Jesus focused on opportunities to strengthen their faith and help them understand more clearly his mission as servant Messiah and their own mission.

A crucial event occurred in Caesarea Philippi. There Jesus asked the disciples who they thought he was, and Peter made his remarkable confession of faith (Matt. 16:13–20). Jesus commended Peter for his recognition of who he was, but he was aware Peter and the others had much more to learn about the nature of his mission and the crisis that lay before him.

Jesus began to speak clearly "from that time on" of the suffering and death that awaited him in Jerusalem (16:21–28). When Peter resisted, the heated exchange between them revealed how little Peter understood about Jesus' destiny as a suffering servant who would die on a cross. Peter did not want Jesus to walk that way, and he and the others were not prepared to take up their own crosses to follow him.

Jesus' words must have been most unsettling to them. They understood his words about suffering and death clearly, but they could not hear his assurance of resurrection and fulfillment to follow. At that time, they needed affirmation of the way of the cross to calm their troubled spirits and give them confidence to continue to believe. Six days later on a high mountain that affirmation came in a most dramatic way.

Interpreting the Scriptures

Jesus' transfiguration was an event of sight and sound beyond normal human experience. The story points to a mystery that defies rational explanation. The value of this event to the disciples and to believers today lies in its affirmation of the unique authority of Jesus and the truth of his prediction of his suffering as the servant Messiah.

The Vision (17:1–4)

17:1. Although this event would bring assurance to all of the disciples, only Peter, James, and John experienced it directly. These three comprised the inner circle of the Twelve. Luke notes Jesus took them up the mountain to pray with him (Luke 9:28). Significantly, these were the three people Jesus later took to be nearest him in Gethsemane, where he prayed before the crucifixion. As witnesses of his heavenly glory on the mountain, they would also be with him as he struggled to face the inevitable cross.

One tradition identifies the "high mountain" as Mount Tabor, a 1,850-foot-high mountain in southern Galilee. Many scholars today think it was more likely Mount Hermon, a 9,100-foot-high peak north of Caesarea Philippi. Mountains are important both in the Old Testament and in Matthew as places of revelation.

17:2. The word *metamorphosis* is derived from the term translated "transfigured." Paul used it in Romans 12:2 to describe the inner spiritual transformation of Christians that enables them to understand and reflect the will of God in their lives. Here, Matthew focused on the dramatic change in Jesus' physical appearance, especially his face, which shone brightly. Upon reflection, the disciples may have recalled the experience of Moses, whose face shone after his meeting with God on Mount Sinai (Exodus 24:15–16; 34:29–35). Jesus' apparel also changed, becoming "dazzling white." The Book of Revelation employs similar expressions to describe heavenly beings or things. The image of the transfigured Jesus may foreshadow the reality of his resurrection in power and glory.

17:3. The scene became more complex as Moses and Elijah appeared and conversed with Jesus. Matthew gave no explanation how the disciples identified them. Neither did he indicate the subject of their conversation. Luke states they were talking about Jesus' "departure," or death, which was to take place in Jerusalem. The conversation confirmed Jesus' own thinking about the meaning of his death.

Interpreters have cited two major reasons these two giants of Jewish heritage appeared with Jesus. Moses, the receiver of the law at Mount Sinai, and Elijah, the first of the prophets of Israel, were fitting representatives of the primary sources of religious authority for the Jews. The law and the prophets held unique importance in the thinking of the covenant people. Jesus' inclusion with these two figures symbolized his own role within the story of God's redemptive action in history. The unfolding event of the transfiguration would affirm Jesus' authority even beyond Israel's most revered revelation of God.

Moses and Elijah also were two people in Jewish history whose departure from earthly life remained shrouded in mystery. The account of Moses' death leaves the place of his burial unknown (Deuteronomy 34:5–6). Later Jewish tradition believed he had not died at all. At the end of Elijah's life, he was taken up by a whirlwind in a chariot of fire into heaven (2 Kings 2:11–12). According to a widely-held tradition, both of these historic leaders in Israel would return before the Messiah came. Their appearance on the mountain with Jesus would confirm this tradition even as it identified Jesus as the long-awaited Messiah.

17:4. Peter's response to the vision revealed his good intentions but lack of understanding. He desired to extend the moment of glory and avoid Jesus' going to Jerusalem to suffer and die, which was for him unthinkable. Peter offered to build "three dwellings," *booths* or *tabernacles*, on the mountain for Jesus, Moses, and Elijah. Perhaps he intended these as a memorial to what had just happened there. He may have envisioned structures which, like the tabernacle in the wilderness, would be a dwelling place for God's glory and presence. He did not have the opportunity to complete his thought or receive a response from Jesus, for the group was arrested by another dramatic event.

The Voice (17:5–8)

A theophany is understood to be a visible and/or audible manifestation of God. Often a theophany comes as a voice from heaven accompanied by unusual and often violent natural phenomena. Clouds, storms, lightning, thunder, darkness, bright light, and wind are typical examples of such phenomena. Although they are rare, the Gospels record theophanies (Matt. 3:16–17; John 12:27–30) at crucial moments in the life and ministry of Jesus. Their purpose was to affirm Jesus in his mission and to commend him to others as worthy of their trust and commitment.

17:5. Clouds often symbolize the presence of God in Scripture. They provide an image that conveys the paradox of God's being both revealed and hidden. As Peter spoke, a "bright cloud" engulfed the mountain. From out of the cloud came a voice that affirmed the unique relationship of Jesus to God and authenticated his authority in the lives of the disciples.

The voice spoke words of assurance that Jesus had heard in the beginning of his ministry at his baptism (Matt. 3:17). In that setting, the words had come primarily for the benefit of Jesus himself. On the mountain of transfiguration, they held special meaning for the disciples' faith and their future ministry. Careful students of the words spoken by the voice have noted reflections from key Old Testament passages. The reference to Jesus as "my Son" reflects Psalm 2:7, a messianic psalm. The words "with whom I am well pleased" echo the words of Isaiah 42:1, one of the four servant songs in Isaiah. The heavenly voice thus speaks of Jesus in terms of sonship and servanthood. The idea of Messiah as servant had been difficult for the disciples to grasp.

The words "listen to him" had special significance in the aftermath of Peter's confession and the experience of the transfiguration. The disciples had difficulty accepting Jesus' instruction about the kind of Messiah he was and the suffering he would have to face. At times they seemed more apt to lecture Jesus than to listen to him. The major purpose of the transfiguration experience was to reinforce the reality of his supreme authority for the disciples and to reaffirm the way of serving and suffering love he had chosen.

17:6–7. The response of the disciples was typical of people throughout the biblical story who encountered God or received divine revelation. They fell back in fear. They were overwhelmed, awestruck. Upon seeing their reaction to the voice, Jesus responded with concern for them. His caring touch and reassuring words, "Do not be afraid," brought them through the moment of crisis.

17:8. The concluding statement that they were alone carries much of the meaning of the experience of the transfiguration. When the disciples lifted their heads, "they saw no one except Jesus himself alone." The representatives of the law and the prophets had disappeared. Jesus stood alone as the sufficient authority and guide for them as they faced the difficult future.

The Struggle to Understand (17:9–13)

Matthew 17:9–13 is difficult for today's reader to interpret. The primary challenge lies in attempting to understand the deeply engrained expectations about the Messiah that had developed for centuries in Jewish tradition. The experience of the transfiguration raised questions in the minds of the disciples as they attempted to reconcile what they had seen and heard with what they had always believed.

17:9. In a strong command, Jesus forbade the disciples from telling what they had seen and heard on the mountain until after the resurrection. What was Jesus' unspoken reason? How could they refrain from sharing such a life-changing experience? Jesus knew his disciples did not yet fully understand the necessity and inevitability of his suffering and death. Even though their vision of the transfigured Jesus had assured them of his ultimate triumph, it appears not to have resolved all their questions about what he said he and they would have to endure. Those who heard the news of the spectacular experience would have had difficulty believing it when the time of Jesus' crucifixion was at hand.

17:10–11. Jesus' mention of the resurrection evidently raised questions in the minds of the disciples based on their understanding of traditional views of eschatology. Based on Malachi 3:1 and 4:5–6, Jewish tradition had developed a detailed understanding of an expected role of Elijah in preparation for the coming of the Messiah. Jesus affirmed the prophecy of Malachi, but he rejected much of the elaborate expectation that had developed from it.

17:12–13. Jesus asserted John the Baptist had come to fulfill Elijah's role as forerunner for the Messiah. Yet, as in the days of the ancient prophets of Israel, many of the people did not recognize John as a prophet or heed his word. Instead, they opposed him and caused him to suffer. Jesus solemnly affirmed that a similar fate awaited him at the hands of the unbelieving people. As the conversation concluded, the disciples understood what Jesus had said about John the Baptist. Whether they believed Jesus is unclear.

Focusing on the Meaning

Discovering the meaning of the story of the transfiguration of Jesus for today can be difficult for many readers. Some may stumble because of questions related to how it occurred and whether it could possibly happen in the real world as we know it. They may have difficulty making willful suspension of disbelief as they read of such phenomena as physical appearances being suddenly transformed, characters long dead present and talking together with those of another era, or the audible voice of God coming from within a cloud. Others may find it difficult to see the possible relevance in tedious disputes over when or whether the prophet Elijah would appear before the coming of the Messiah. The story can sound strange in the ears of many who hear it today for the first time. What can it mean for us?

The transfiguration experience, like the resurrection itself, authenticates Jesus' insistence that the way to glory is the way of serving and suffering. Throughout Jesus' life he faced the temptation to seek power and glory by avoiding this difficult way, but he resisted the temptation. Some have expressed Jesus' conviction as *no cross, no crown*. Even in achieving lesser goals, we know the value of demanding discipline and cite the familiar truism, "No pain, no gain!"

What is seen as defeat in the eyes of the world may, in reality, be the seed of great victory. A noted historian reflecting on what he had learned in a lifetime of studying history said one of his most important discoveries was the defeat of victory and the victory of defeat. He cited the cross of Jesus as the supreme example of this truth.

The transfiguration affirms the supremacy of the authority of Jesus above any others. In our culture of competing causes and authorities that demand our loyalty, we need to experience the reality of seeing Jesus himself alone and listening only to him.

TEACHING PLANS

Teaching Plan—Varied Learning Activities

Connect with Life

1. Give each member of the class a pen and sheet of paper. Encourage each person to write a brief note of affirmation to someone. Allow the class to read their notes if they wish. Share a personal story of how someone affirmed you through words or a note. Tell of the impact that experience had on your life.

2. Tell a personal story of a time when someone encouraged you in the faith. Perhaps it happened when Jesus saved you or at a crucial time in your life. Invite others to share similar stories when someone affirmed them in their faith. As an option, invite a church staff member to tell how someone affirmed him or her when he or she accepted the call into ministry. Discuss the role of affirmation in our spiritual development.

Guide Bible Study

3. Summarize Matthew 13—16 to set the context for the focal passage for this lesson by doing these things:

   a. Read Matthew 13:24–30. Select people to pantomime the story as you read. The characters should include the person sowing seeds, the enemy, the servants, the weeds, and the wheat. Assign people to fill these roles.

   b. Do the same with the parable of the net in Matthew 13:47–50. The characters should include the anglers, the good fish, and the bad fish.

   c. Direct the class to the stories of Jesus' feeding the five thousand (Matt. 14:13–21), walking on water (14:22), receiving Peter's confession (16:13), and predicting his death (16:21). Invite discussion of Matthew's possible reasons for including these parables and events. Point out that Matthew was painting a picture of Jesus as the Messiah.

4. Borrow a toy *Transformer* from a child to use to illustrate the word *transfiguration*. (Ask the child to demonstrate the toy before you attempt to transform it in class.) Explain that the Greek word for *transfiguration* literally means *transformed or dramatically altered*. Ask the students to name other items that can transform from one state to another. Read Matthew 17:2. Ask, *What do you think is the significance to the change in Jesus' face and clothes?* Enlist a person to read Exodus 24:15–16; 34:29–35 and Matthew 28:3. After reading these texts, ask the question again regarding Jesus' appearance.

5. Form two groups (no more than six people in each group). Give each group a sheet of poster board and markers. (Also provide a Bible dictionary, study Bible, concordance, or similar Bible study resources for each group if possible.) Select one group to write significant facts about Moses and his life. Instruct the other group to write significant facts about Elijah and his life. Display the poster boards, and ask each group to discuss their character. Lead the class in a discussion of the significance of Moses' and Elijah's appearance on the mount of transfiguration. Read Deuteronomy 18:15 and Malachi 4:5–6 to aid in the discussion.

6. Form three groups, one group to represent Jesus, one group to represent Peter, and one group to represent James and John. Give each group a Bible, pen, and sheet of paper. Ask each group to read Matthew 17:1–13 and prepare a monologue telling the story from their character's vantage point. Allow each group to read their monologue. Lead the class in a discussion using the following questions.

   a. Why did Jesus take only three disciples to the mount? Why these three?

   b. Can you name another time when Jesus took only Peter, James, and John with him? (Matt. 26:36–38)

   c. What do you think might be the connection between these two passages?

   d. Why did Peter want to build three dwellings? (See "Bible Comments" on 17:4 in this *Teaching Guide* and comments on 17:1–4 in the *Study Guide*.)

   e. Why do you think Jesus wanted the disciples to wait until the resurrection to tell what happened?

Encourage Application

7. Read Matthew 16:24–26. State that all the disciples had a hard time accepting that Jesus must suffer. On the markerboard write this heading: "What Jesus' transfiguration means for my life." Ask people to turn to two people next to them and identify one or two thoughts about what Jesus' transfiguration means for our lives today. Receive reports afterward. Be certain to mention that God's affirmation of Jesus' life of service and sacrifice calls for us to live as Jesus lived.

8. Pray for each member by name. Ask God to encourage each person this week.

Teaching Plan—Lecture and Questions

Connect with Life

1. Before the session, write the following sentences on separate sheets of paper and hang them on a wall. "Mary, you have found favor _____ _____" (Luke 1:28, NIV)."Well done, good _____ _____ _____" (Matt. 25:21, NIV). "This is my Son, _____ _____ _____ _____ _____ _____" (Matt. 3:17, NIV). "We always thank God, the Father of our Lord Jesus Christ, when we pray for you, because we have heard of _____ _____ _____ _____ _____ and of the love you have for all the saints" (Colossians 1:3–4). Lead the class in completing the verses.

Guide Bible Study

2. Lead a brief discussion of the background in Matthew 13—16. Use the information under "From Parables to the Transfiguration" in the *Study Guide* and "Understanding the Context" in this *Teaching Guide* to determine talking points. Inform the class that beginning in chapter 13, Matthew focused intently on the life of Jesus as Jesus began to move toward the cross. Sketch a timeline on the markerboard to show Matthew's progression. Include the following points on the timeline: Jesus teaches in parables (13:1–52); Jesus teaches in his hometown (13:53–58); John the Baptist is beheaded (14:1–12); Jesus feeds the five thousand (14:13–21); Jesus walks on water (14:22–33); Peter confesses Christ (16:13–20); Jesus predicts his death (16:21–28).

3. Read Matthew 17:1–2. Lead a discussion on the meaning of Jesus' appearance changing during the transfiguration. Ask the class to list occasions in the Bible when a person's appearance changed. Discuss what those changes meant in each case listed. Read Exodus 24:15–16 and 34:29–35 to add to the discussion.

4. Read Matthew 17:3–4. Ask: *What are some possible reasons Peter wanted to build three shelters?* List the answers on a markerboard. Remind the class of Peter's words in Matthew 16:22, and discuss

the correlation between Peter's two statements. Ask: *Why was it difficult for Peter and the other disciples to accept that Jesus must die?* Ask the class to respond to this statement: *The disciples had difficulty accepting that Jesus must suffer because they were afraid that they too must suffer.*

5. Read the following case study and invite discussion:

    Joel invited his friend Carlos to church. Carlos recently moved to town and wanted to find a new church. Carlos was active in his former church and was eager to find another church where he could serve. Joel was excited about his growing church and wanted Carlos to meet his pastor and experience a worship service. Carlos joined Joel for worship and immediately loved the music and the environment. The preacher was enthusiastic and passionate. However, as Carlos listened to the pastor he heard things like this: trust in God and you will never worry about money again. The preacher exclaimed that if a person followed Jesus that person would never get sick, would have plenty of money, and would never get depressed or anxious about anything again. In fact, the preacher said that Jesus would make a person's dreams come true. If you were Carlos, what would you do? How would you respond to the message?

Encourage Application

6. Read Matthew 16:24–26 and 17:9, 11–12. Ask: *What do these thoughts mean for followers of Christ today? Did Jesus' death and resurrection put an end to Christian suffering? What do you think God's affirmation at the transfiguration of Jesus' way, the way of the cross, means for us today?* Close by praying for one another.

FOCAL TEXT
Matthew 26:26–30;
27:11–14, 35–50

BACKGROUND
Matthew 26—27

MAIN IDEA
Jesus was faithful to his
mission to the point
of giving his life.

QUESTION TO EXPLORE
What does Jesus' giving his
life tell us about the kind
of disciples we are to be?

TEACHING AIM
To lead adults to decide
how they will respond to
the message that the Son of
God gave his life for them

LESSON ELEVEN
Giving His Life

UNIT FOUR
Hope in Jesus'
Glorification

BIBLE COMMENTS

Understanding the Context

The journey of Jesus and his disciples from the transfiguration (Matthew 17:1–13) to Jerusalem revealed the striking contrast between Jesus' commitment to what awaited him there and the disciples' resistance to the inevitable cross. Matthew's narrative contains much dialog as Jesus interpreted the meaning of events along the way and focused on preparing the disciples for the difficult days that lay before them. Several key themes emerge in Matthew's account.

First, Jesus remained undeterred from his destiny to die on the cross, even though the disciples sought to turn him from it. He continued to speak clearly about his suffering and death as fulfillment of his mission as the servant Messiah. The disciples could not understand or accept the idea that the Messiah would give his life rather than exercise his power to overcome his enemies.

A second theme on this journey reflects Jesus' continuing concern for the disciples' future. He taught them about the implications of the way they were called to follow. He dealt with issues concerning their relationships with others and the importance of forgiveness. In recounting the last journey to Jerusalem, Matthew recorded the final two major discourses of the five he included in his Gospel: Jesus' sermon on the church (Matt. 18:1–35) and his eschatological teaching (24:1—25:46).

During the final journey, Jesus' clashes with the religious leaders became more intense. In his ministry of healing and teaching, the Pharisees found many occasions to question him harshly. As he arrived in Jerusalem, Jesus evoked public acclaim through the triumphal entry into the city and later his cleansing of the temple. These actions, however, provoked his opponents to take drastic steps to plot his destruction.

As Jesus and his disciples prepared to observe their last Passover meal together, a disturbing subplot was developing. Judas met with Jewish authorities to plan for his becoming an accomplice in Jesus' arrest. The undercurrent of Judas's impending betrayal and the disciples' predicted desertion created a unique emotional context for their final celebration of Passover with Jesus. During the meal, Jesus confronted the group with a painful reality: "One of you will betray me" (26:21). Jesus' assertion provoked both protest and painful self-doubt in the disciples.

Interpreting the Scriptures

The Lord's Supper (26:26–30)

Compare Matthew's account with Mark 14:22–25, Luke 22:14–23, and 1 Corinthians 11:17–34 for a full understanding of the basis of the Christian observance of the Lord's Supper. Matthew's account emphasizes the Lord's Supper as an expression of thanksgiving, a symbol of a new covenant, and an affirmation of Jesus' death as a sacrifice for the forgiveness of sin.

26:26. Jesus took a loaf of the unleavened bread prepared for the Passover meal and blessed it. Literally, *He said the blessing.* He broke the loaf and gave bread to his disciples. To refer to *breaking bread* is a way of saying to eat together. The action here points to the Lord's Supper as an expression of communion or fellowship among the disciples.

The statement "this is my body" identifies Jesus with the bread of the Passover meal. Reflecting on the broken bread, Christians have seen it as a continuing symbol of the incarnation, the word made flesh in Jesus (see John 1:1–14). In sharing the bread together, believers reflect their identity with Christ and with one another.

Christians have treasured Jesus' simple act and symbolic words, even as they have often strongly disagreed about their precise meaning. Unfortunately in Christian history, deep divisions in the church have come as believers have attempted to understand whether the bread is a symbol of Christ's body, whether it becomes the body of Christ, or whether it embodies Christ's real presence.

26:27–28. Jesus also took the cup prepared for the Passover meal and gave thanks. Many Christians refer to the Lord's Supper as the Eucharist, which is derived from the Greek term used here for giving thanks. Jesus invited all the disciples to drink from the cup. The word "all" refers to the disciples rather than the contents of the cup.

Jesus related the historical meaning of the Passover cup to himself. The cup represented his blood, and it became a symbol of his life given to fulfill his saving purpose. Jesus referred to the cup as the "blood of the covenant." Some Greek manuscripts insert the word for *new* before "covenant" to characterize the new relationship binding God and humankind that was made possible through Jesus' giving his life in death on the cross. Jesus' words call to mind the promise of a new covenant in Jeremiah 31:31–34.

26:28. Jesus' blood was "poured out," depicting life freely given. Jesus, especially in John's Gospel, spoke of laying down his life rather than its being taken from him (see John 10:14).

Jesus saw his death as being in behalf of others. The phrase "for many" includes all who would respond in faith to this great gift. Jesus' words reflected the promise of the servant's mission in Isaiah 53:11. The word "many" is not restrictive, that is, it refers not only to some, but to all. Jesus connected his death to the forgiveness of sin. It was sacrificial, having the effect of removing the barrier of sin that separates humanity from God.

26:29–30. The symbols of the bread and wine were to be continuing somber reminders of the reality of Jesus' death. They were also to become symbols of hope. Jesus affirmed that the results of his giving his life were the forgiveness of sin and reconciliation with God. He pointed the disciples to the time of the full realization of the kingdom of God. He would partake of the cup again with them in the messianic feast that celebrated that event.

Jesus and the disciples next departed to the Garden of Gethsemane on the Mount of Olives for a time of continued reflection and prayer. He reiterated his prediction the disciples would all become deserters. Although they resisted Jesus' words, the apostles soon would demonstrate their truth as they abandoned him. Matthew's account of events between the Passover meal and the trials of Jesus shows the dramatic difference between the constancy of Jesus' commitment to face his destiny and the fear and flight of the disciples. Even Peter was to follow him at a distance and ultimately deny being Jesus' disciple.

Standing Strong in Trial (27:11–14)

27:11–12. The Jewish religious leaders sought to get rid of Jesus because he made the claim to be one with God. Their religious concerns, however, had little effect in the realm of Roman justice. To bring about the death of Jesus, these leaders charged him with sedition. They said he claimed to be a king, thus making him a threat to the authority of Rome. Even though there was no evidence to indicate Jesus desired to foment revolution against Rome, the authorities who sat nervously in the seats of power took such charges seriously.

When Pilate asked Jesus whether he were guilty of the charge against him, Jesus responded in a way that appears to acknowledge the title without accepting Pilate's understanding of its meaning. Beyond this, Jesus did not respond to any of the particular accusations. His silence demonstrated his integrity and his profound dependence on God. "When he was abused, he did not return abuse; when he suffered, he did not threaten; but he entrusted himself to the one who judges justly" (1 Peter 2:23).

27:13–14. Pilate was amazed at the poise of Jesus and his persistent silence. Pilate's words indicate he did not really consider Jesus a threat to Rome, and he was impressed by one who demonstrated such strength in such difficult circumstances. Yet, the pressure of the crowd was more persuasive to Pilate than his own conscience. Although he did not consider Jesus to be a threat to him, an unruly populace could be. To quiet the crowd, he went along with the charade of justice.

The Taunting Crowd (27:35–44)

27:35–36. Crucifixion was a horrible method of execution to which the Roman soldiers had evidently become insensitive. Completing their awful task, they cast lots at the foot of the cross to see who would receive the clothing of Jesus as the spoils of their despicable labor. The experience of being placed on the cross was painful. The agony of the long hours of suffering there before death came was excruciating. The soldiers were to keep watch at the cross until Jesus died.

27:37. The accusation against Jesus was placed as a written notice on the cross. Perhaps Pilate intended the inscription "the King of the Jews" to mock both Jesus and the Jews. Ironically, what was intended as either a routine display of the charges that resulted in crucifixion or a cruel slap at Jesus and the Jews proved to be true. He was the Anointed One of Israel who came to his throne by way of the cross. Neither the Romans nor the Jews could understand this.

27:39–40. In addition to the physical suffering Jesus endured, his death was made more difficult by the jeers of the taunting crowd. The soldiers had mocked him prior to the crucifixion. The crowds jeered, and the chief priests and other religious leaders mocked him. Even the two bandits who were crucified alongside Jesus joined in the ridicule.

From the time of the wilderness temptations, Jesus had heard the tempter's voice urging him to avoid the way of the cross. Here it came in the words of those who taunted him: "save yourself." Even Jesus' closest disciples sought to turn him from his course that would take him to Jerusalem to die.

27:41–43. The taunts of the religious leaders reflected their dual charges that Jesus claimed to be the King of the Jews and the Son of God. The assumption of those who taunted Jesus was if he could not save himself, he could not possibly save anyone else. Ironically, however, he could not save others if he *did* save himself. Salvation for humanity could come only through God's self-giving love. Without such self-sacrifice, there could be no redeeming power. The issue was not his possession of divine power but his commitment to a redemptive purpose. The only way to save others was through a costly commitment of sacrificial love.

27:44. The thieves joined in the taunting. See Luke 23:32–43 for the account of the thief who repented and asked for Jesus' mercy.

The Final Moments (27:45–50)

27:45. Jesus endured his final hours in darkness. The darkening of the sun noted by Matthew suggests more than a merely natural phenomenon. It sets the mood for the deep sense of separation and suffering that marked Jesus' death.

27:46. Jesus was sustained on the cross by his faith in God, even when it appeared he had been abandoned by God. There is a depth to the mystery of his suffering that is impenetrable by human reason. The sacrifice of the righteous for the unrighteous, the sinless for the sinful, seems both unjust and impossible. The agony of enduring the consequences of others' sins can only be partially realized in human experience.

Jesus appears to have found sustenance from the Scriptures in the moment of deepest darkness. His cry of dereliction is expressed in the words of Psalm 22:1. The psalm opens with a cry of anguish but ends in a song of praise. Perhaps in his agony, Jesus drew strength from this witness that the times when God seems far away can be preparation for the revelation of God's presence and power. The cry of abandonment can become the preface to praise.

The cry of dereliction comprises the only words of Jesus from the cross recorded by Matthew and Mark. Luke and John each include others.

27:47–49. Some in the crowd misunderstood Jesus' words as a call to Elijah to save him. Seeing Jesus in agony prompted someone to get a sponge dipped in wine to give to him. Whether this was an act of human compassion or a further act of humiliation is unclear. Some counseled waiting to see whether Elijah would come to Jesus' rescue.

27:50. Jesus "cried again with a loud voice." Matthew does not indicate whether this was the expression of words or simply the cry of pain. John records that Jesus' last words were in effect a shout of triumph, "It is finished!" (John 19:30).

Jesus "breathed his last." Another translation is "he gave up his spirit" (NRSV margin), which may indicate this as a voluntary action. Whether this is conveyed by the language, it is clear throughout the last days of Jesus' life he saw his death as a matter of his obedience to God and the fulfillment of his mission.

Focusing on the Meaning

God was acting in a unique way in Christ to reconcile the world to himself. This understanding of the cross has always been difficult for people to hear and accept. Paul said that the preaching of the cross was heard by some as a stumbling block, a sign of defeat and weakness. Others heard the message as foolishness, making no sense in a rational world. To those who believe, however, the cross of Christ was and is the source and symbol of our salvation.

Jesus gave his life voluntarily in response to the will of God. He became a voluntary victim, accepting the consequences of others' sins and bearing suffering he did not deserve. Throughout the events of his last days, Jesus demonstrated a sense of calmness and control that were unusual for someone in such circumstances. Although he was violently opposed by religious and civil authorities, he in effect gave his life willingly in commitment to God's redemptive purpose for all humankind.

Jesus' death provided something for us we could never obtain for ourselves. The early Christians understood the death of Jesus in sacrificial terms. He died as a sacrifice for the sins of humankind that separate us from God. The cross is the expression of God's gift of grace, freely given to restore us to fellowship with God.

Jesus' giving of himself for us evokes a response that leads us to give our lives to serve him and others. The self-giving love of Jesus can become contagious in those who receive his grace and determine to pass it on. The great hymn by Isaac Watts, "When I Survey the Wondrous Cross," expresses the authentic response of those who have experienced the wonder of God's great love for us: "Were the whole realm of nature mine, That were a present far too small. Love so amazing, so divine, Demands my soul, my life, my all!"

TEACHING PLANS

Teaching Plan—Varied Learning Activities

Connect with Life

1. Before the session arrange the room so that the class is seated around a table or tables. Prepare a plate of bread and a pitcher of

grape juice for each table. Begin by referring to the comments in the introduction to the lesson in the *Study Guide* about a life mission statement. Ask whether the class has thought about their own life mission and whether they have formulated a statement that guides their life. Invite comments, but if people do not choose to respond, do not press. Continuing by asking whether the group thinks having a life mission statement would be helpful. Point out that the events to be studied today have such significance that they need to be at the heart of our understanding of our life mission, whether we write down a statement or not.

Guide Bible Study

2. Inform the class that the Scriptures you study today fulfill the purpose of the Scriptures studied in the previous lesson. Remind the group that the last session examined the transfiguration of Jesus, when God made the bold statement that he was pleased with Jesus and his obedience. In this session, we will read that Jesus' obedience to follow God's plan caused him to die. Write the words "Follower of Christ" on a markerboard. Invite the class to share their thoughts and understanding of these words by asking, *What do they mean? How does a person become a "follower of Christ"?* Write responses on the markerboard.

3. Enlist someone to read Matthew 26:26–30 while the class listens for the instructions Jesus gave the disciples in these verses ("Take and eat; this is my body"; "Drink from it, all of you," NIV). Refer to the bread, and remind the class that the bread symbolizes Jesus' body given for our sins. Refer to the juice, and remind the class that the juice symbolizes Jesus' blood shed for the forgiveness of our sins. Read Matthew 26:28 again, and ask the group to comment on what Jesus meant by the "blood of the covenant." Refer as needed to the information about this topic under "Mission Possible" in the *Study Guide.*

4. Lead the class in a time of silent reflection, encouraging the class to focus on Jesus' suffering and death. After a few minutes, as the class continues in a time of reflection, read Matthew 27:11–14. Ask: *Why do you think Jesus remained silent as the religious leaders*

falsely accused him? Why is it difficult to remain silent when falsely accused? What did Jesus' silence communicate about his purpose?

5. Give a sheet of paper and a pen to each member. Instruct the class to write down observations and significant statements as you read Matthew 27:35–50. Discuss a few of the statements recorded by the class. On the markerboard, write the words, "*Eloi, Eloi, lama sabachthani?*" Ask the class members to share their thoughts about these words Jesus used. Inquire, *What is your reaction to these words?* Using information under the heading "Results Worth Your Life" in the *Study Guide* and in "Bible Comments" in this *Teaching Guide,* lead in a discussion regarding possible meaning of Jesus' words.

6. Divide the class into teams. Provide for each team poster board, markers, and a study Bible with center column references or other study helps. Instruct the teams to examine Matthew 27:35–50 to identify the details or statements about the crucifixion that are found in the Old Testament. (If time is limited, divide the Scriptures into sections, and assign a section to each team.) Instruct each team to write the Old Testament Scripture verse and the prophecy on the poster board. Discuss each team's findings, and attach the posters to a wall.

Encourage Application

7. Ask the class to survey the focal passages again, looking for how various people responded to Jesus' giving his life on the cross. Note ideas on the markerboard. Ask, *What do the passages suggest about the best way to respond?* Refer to the hymn by Isaac Watts, "When I Survey the Wondrous Cross." Read one or two of the stanzas, but especially the closing stanza. Encourage the class to consider whether they have responded with their life, their all. Encourage them to do so if they have not. Indicate your willingness to talk with anyone who wishes to explore this further.

8. Find an advertisement in a local or national newspaper or magazine seeking to fill positions. Read it to the class or make copies. Ask the class to help you adapt the advertisement to make it into

a description for a follower Christ. Jot down ideas on the board. After coming to a consensus, ask someone to write it down. Work with that person to e-mail it to each participant during the coming week.

Teaching Plan—Lecture and Questions

Connect with Life

1. Begin the class by asking the group to share mission statements or slogans they know.[1] Write these on a markerboard. Ask volunteers whether anyone has a personal mission statement. If so, invite them to share it if they wish.

2. Before the session, enlist two class members to research and present to the class two stories about two people who gave their lives for something they believed in (or you could research and present these yourself).[2] Ask: *What were the results of these people giving their lives? What is something or someone you would consider worthy for which to give your life? How can we determine whether something is worth dying for?*

Guide Bible Study

3. Ask: *How would you state what Jesus' earthly mission was?* Write ideas on a markerboard. Lead in a discussion on various events that attempted to distract Jesus from his mission. Use the temptation of Jesus found in Matthew 4:1–11 as an example.

4. Invite someone to read Matthew 26:26–30 while the class listens for what this passage tells us about Jesus' mission. Receive comments. Ask: *Why was it difficult for Jesus' disciples to understand these statements about his death?*

5. Using the information under "Mission Possible" in the *Study Guide* and in "Bible Comments" in this *Teaching Guide*, give a brief lecture on the scriptural idea of covenant. Ask: *Why did Jesus say his blood was the blood of the covenant?*

6. Enlist someone to read Matthew 27:11–14. Ask, *Why did Jesus answer the governor when he asked him whether he was king of the Jews but remain silent when the chief priests and elders accused him? What did Jesus' silence communicate to the governor? What did it communicate to his accusers? What does it communicate to us?* Lead a brief discussion of the power of silence in the midst of false accusation. Guide the discussion by asking the class to respond to the following statement, "Silence is golden." Explain these verses further as needed, using information in the *Study Guide* and "Bible Comments" in this *Teaching Guide.*

7. Call for someone to read Matthew 27:35–50 while the class listens closely to what Jesus experienced. Lead the class to share how they felt as you read these verses. Ask, *In addition to the physical pain, what are other ways Jesus suffered on the cross?*

Encourage Application

8. Ask, *How do these verses that deal with the Last Supper and the events of the cross make you feel? What is the best way of responding to these verses?* Remind the class that a response is called for by each person. Encourage the group to decide to follow Jesus or follow him more closely. Refer to the Question to Explore, "What does Jesus' giving his life tell us about the kind of disciples we are to be?" Call for responses.

9. Close in a time of prayer thanking Jesus for his willingness to suffer for his people. Ask God for courage to follow Jesus.

NOTES

1. For example: Dell computers—To be the most successful computer company in the world at delivering the best customer experience in markets we serve; Microsoft—To help people and businesses throughout the world reach their potential; Chick-Fil-A—To be America's best quick-service restaurant.

2. Examples: Lottie Moon (see /www.sbhla.org/bio_moon.htm);
John Bunyan (see www.christianitytoday.com/history/special/131christians/bunyan.html);
Bill Wallace, Baptist missionary (see www.wmbc.net/templates/cuswallace/
details.asp?id=31704&PID=322415). Each site was accessed 7/28/08.

FOCAL TEXT
Matthew 28:1–10, 16–20

BACKGROUND
Matthew 28

MAIN IDEA
The crucified and now
resurrected Christ commands
his followers to make
disciples of all people.

QUESTION TO EXPLORE
What does "make disciples"
mean, and what do we need
to do to be more faithful in
carrying out Jesus' command?

TEACHING AIM
To lead adults to describe what
"make disciples" means and
decide on actions they will
take to be more faithful in
carrying out Jesus' command

LESSON TWELVE

Under the Command of the Resurrected Christ

UNIT FOUR

Hope in Jesus' Glorification

BIBLE COMMENTS

Understanding the Context

Enduring the *in-between* times can be one of the more difficult challenges of life. When people experience great loss and the way forward is not yet clear, the sense of life's purpose is elusive. When high expectations lie shattered, it is difficult to dream again. When hope is gone, the counsel to live one day at a time is tough to follow. Commitment to mission easily gives way to a struggle to survive.

Jesus attempted to prepare his disciples for the reality they did not want to face. He not only spoke clearly about the cross that lay before him but also assured them of the hope that lay beyond his death. The disciples had difficulty accepting the bad news and did not seem to hear or remember the good news at all. Each of the Gospels focuses on the final week of Jesus' life, as events rapidly unfolded in ways that left no doubt Jesus' predictions were coming true.

Matthew reveals the toll these events took on the faith and fellowship of the disciples. Only the women continued to express their love and loyalty consistently during the final days. The prediction by Jesus of the desertion of all his disciples (Matthew 26:31–32) is especially significant for understanding some of the post-resurrection events. The stories of Judas's betrayal and Peter's denial in the courtyard of the high priest are well-known. Perhaps as important was the silent slipping away of the others, leaving Jesus to face arrest, trial, and death with few to support him.

The Gospels do not describe the disciples' experience during the dark days between Jesus' crucifixion and the resurrection in great detail. We know they gathered together to share their grief and seek to overcome their fear. We know from the reflection of the two people on the road to Emmaus they felt disillusionment and despair. We know that some, like Thomas, had to deal with the reality of Jesus' death in personal and private ways.

Interpreting the Scriptures

The Startling Discovery (28:1–4)

28:1. Mary Magdalene and "the other Mary" dealt with their grief by coming to Jesus' tomb at dawn on resurrection morning. They were the last people at the cross on the day of crucifixion and the first at the tomb on the day of resurrection. Compelled by love, they came to do what they could to honor Jesus' body. Mark stated they had brought spices to anoint Jesus' body for appropriate burial (Mark 16:1). Although the crucifixion had destroyed their hopes and battered their faith, it had not changed their enduring love for Jesus.

28:2–3. The women were not prepared for what they discovered when they arrived. Matthew states that a mighty earthquake occurred and an angel descended to roll away the large stone that had sealed the tomb. The angel not only opened the tomb but also remained to interpret what had happened. Angels are messengers of God, and this one had history's most important announcement to deliver. His radiant and brilliant white clothing signaled his heavenly origin. The description of his apparel is similar to that of Jesus' garments at the transfiguration.

28:4. The initial reaction of those who experienced the immediate aftermath of the resurrection was fear. The guards, who were there because they had to be, and the women, who were there because they wanted to be, were both overcome by fear. The guards "became like dead men." They were paralyzed with fright. Undoubtedly the guards knew the potential consequences of failing to carry out their responsibility. Beyond their terror of the moment, they feared what would most likely lie ahead, their execution.

An Invitation and Command (28:5–7)

28:5. Often the words "do not be afraid" are the first words of angels in Scripture to anxious human beings. Evidently the women did not expect to hear good news from a heavenly messenger. Fear can rivet our attention to the trouble and terror of the moment and cause us to lose the larger perspective provided by memory and hope.

28:6. The mission of angels includes the responsibility to remind us of what we already know. Jesus had been raised, "as he said." Jesus had told them, but in their fear and grief they had forgotten. The end of the story would be triumph over tragedy. Their fear would be dispelled by the promise of Jesus' living presence that nothing could take away.

The stone had been rolled away, not to let Jesus out, but to let his followers in. The empty tomb was one part of the evidence Christ was alive. It not only helped to convince the skeptics, but it was also useful to reassure doubting and fearful followers. The angel invited the women to look in and see that Jesus was no longer in the grave. It was an invitation to assurance.

28:7. The invitation to "come, see the place where he lay" was followed by a command to "go quickly and tell" the disciples what they had seen. Such a momentous discovery could not be kept to themselves but had to be shared. People become stewards of their experiences of grace. The women, who had come to the tomb in sorrow to express devotion even death could not kill, left in joy to declare the good news of a living Lord to his disciples.

The women were to tell the disciples Jesus "is going ahead of you to Galilee," and assure them he would see them there. The phrase "going ahead of you" could be translated *leading you*. The expression is used in the Bible to picture a shepherd's leading a flock of sheep. This message would have reminded the disciples of Jesus' painful prediction on the night of Passover that all of the disciples would desert him and be scattered like sheep without a shepherd. He had also said, "But after I am raised up, I will go ahead of you to Galilee" (26:31–32). Their desertion would break their fellowship, but after the resurrection the fellowship would be renewed.

An important feature in the story is the strategic role played by women. Mary Magdalene and Mary became the first people to proclaim the news of the resurrection. In first-century Jewish culture, the testimony of women was not admissible in court proceedings and their role in religious matters was limited. This may have contributed to the reluctance of some disciples to believe their story, which they considered to be "an idle tale" (Luke 24:11). The women proved to be both faithful in their devotion to Jesus and responsible in bearing witness to the resurrection.

An Unexpected Encounter (28:8–10)

28:8. Mary Magdalene and Mary followed the instruction of the angel eagerly. They left "quickly" and "ran" to find the disciples and tell them the news. Matthew provides insight into their inner feelings in saying they left "with fear and great joy." Entrusted with so great a task, they would understandably feel both exhilaration and apprehension.

28:9. Obedience to the angel's command brought the women an even more profound religious experience. On the road of obedience, they encountered the risen Christ himself. Jesus spoke a customary word translated simply, "Greetings!" This may appear rather perfunctory in the unusual circumstances. The literal meaning of the word, *rejoice,* may be a more appropriate expression for the occasion. The women responded by kneeling and grasping Jesus' feet, offering to him their worship. Their actions acknowledged his Lordship in awe and wonder.

28:10. Jesus responded by calming their fears and repeating the command the angel gave them. Note a change in that Jesus used the phrase "my brothers" rather than "disciples" (28:7). Although they had deserted him, he still affirmed his close relationship to them.

A Commission to Make Disciples (28:16–20)

28:16. The disciples assembled in Galilee in response to the women's message. Note that they went to "the mountain," the first mention of this detail in the story. Note again the significance of mountains in Matthew's Gospel as places of revelation. Although the specific mountain in Galilee is not named, some interpreters see that this may have been the location of Jesus' Sermon on the Mount at the beginning of his ministry (Matt. 5:1). Others think it may have been the place where he commissioned the disciples for their earlier Galilean mission (10:1).

28:17. The meeting enabled the disciples to express their adoration, resolve their lingering doubts, and receive their commission to bear witness to their crucified and risen Lord. This mountaintop experience, like most of the recorded spiritual experiences in the Bible, was to prepare people for a task to be done. Authentic worship inevitably results in mission. The mountaintop of revelation is to prepare one for the valley of service.

28:18. Throughout his ministry, Jesus assumed the right to command. Earlier Jesus claimed "all things have been handed over to me by my Father" (11:27). In this final meeting with the disciples, Jesus asserted he had been given "all authority in heaven and on earth." The authority of his presence during his ministry was reinforced and extended by his experience of the cross and the resurrection. In raising Jesus from the dead, God had vindicated his life and validated his words. His authority was adequate to empower his followers for mission.

28:19. The commission to the disciples was to make other disciples. They were to reach people with the news of what God had done and was doing in Jesus, the risen Christ, with the intent they would also become his followers. Becoming a disciple meant beginning a life of learning the teachings of Jesus and applying them faithfully.

The word "nations" can be translated as *peoples*. Jews who spoke Greek used the term to speak of the Gentiles. Jesus' command focused primarily on people groups rather than political entities or merely geographical extension of the movement. Note that this commission removed the restrictions placed on the disciples as they embarked on the earlier Galilean mission. At that time, Jesus forbade their going among the Gentiles and sent them specifically "to the lost sheep of the house of Israel" (10:6).

Witnesses for the crucified and risen Christ have as their goal reaching people who will openly declare their faith through the act of baptism. In baptism, new believers take to themselves the name of the living God who created them in love, redeemed them through the work of the Son, and is powerfully and personally with them in the Holy Spirit. Baptism is not a perfunctory ritual, but an enacted parable of the drama of redemption. It is an abiding symbol of the life-changing power of a relationship to the living Christ.

28:20. Christ's witnesses are to help people recognize the implications of their new faith in daily life. Discipleship involves not only profession of faith but also the practice of faithfulness in the way of Christ. "Teaching them to obey everything I have commanded you," has always been the most difficult part of the commission to carry out. The form of the word "teaching" indicates it is a continuing process throughout the life of the disciple. The goal of the one who makes disciples is not to enable people to know more but to enable them to reflect the character of Christ daily.

The Great Commission of the resurrected Christ calls for greater resources than anyone has. Jesus knew the disciples' greatest need would be the sense of his empowering presence. Jesus promised he would be with them "always," literally *all the days*. The literal reading suggests the presence of the risen Christ day by day, providing the resources for each day's need. The Gospel, which begins with the promise of the coming of Emmanuel, God with us (Matt.1:23), concludes with the assurance the One who came will never leave us.

Focusing on the Meaning

Matthew's account of the aftermath of the resurrection focuses on the two themes that became the primary evidence for the early Christian witness to the risen Christ. The tomb was empty, and Jesus appeared to his disciples. Although one cannot establish an exact chronology from the varied resurrection stories, each Gospel emphasizes the effect of these two facts on the disciples. Jesus' followers were ready to quit after the cross. Following their encounters with the risen Christ, they came to accept an overwhelming responsibility to make disciples of all people throughout the world.

The experience of the disciples provides clues for all believers to come to see the Great Commission of Jesus as applying to themselves as well. Within the study passage one can discover what it takes to carry out the commission to make disciples effectively.

- One who makes disciples must have an experience of the risen Christ. People cannot share what they do not have. The dispirited disciples demonstrate the necessity of the continuing empowering presence of Christ.
- Disciple-makers demonstrate the willingness to obey the command of the risen Christ. The earliest Christian confession of faith was "Jesus Christ is Lord." To make this confession was to accept Christ's authority.
- Effective disciple-makers have confidence in the truth of the message they proclaim and teach. They continue to learn of Christ

and discover the relevance of his teaching for themselves in daily life.

- Faithful witnesses to Christ have a sense of urgency in the conviction that all people need the Lord. Although they may not sense a call to go to distant lands and people, they recognize that the people who are within the scope of their daily activities need Christ. They become sensitive to ways their words and deeds can bring others to know and follow Christ.
- People who make disciples take seriously Jesus' command to teach new followers to apply all of his teachings to all of life. Making a disciple and becoming a disciple are lifelong tasks that require continuing commitment.

TEACHING PLANS

Teaching Plan—Varied Learning Activities

Connect with Life

1. Write "Disciple" vertically on a markerboard in order to prepare to lead the class in developing an acrostic from the word. Ask the class to use the letters in the word *disciple* to think of words that describe a disciple of Jesus. For example, *D – devoted*. Write these words on the markerboard. Read Matthew 28:18–20. Ask what these verses are generally called (Great Commission) Note that the task given to the Eleven was to "make disciples." Explain the word *commission* using this definition, "A job, or task given to a person or a group, especially an order to produce a particular product or piece of work." Lead the class to discuss how this definition connects to the Great Commission.

Guide Bible Study

2. Review briefly Matthew 27. Use the information in this chapter to provide the background for the events of Matthew 28. Point out that Jesus fulfilled his mission to die for the sins of the world. Too, God had fulfilled his mission to raise Jesus from the dead. Now, Jesus gives his followers a mission to tell the world about him.

3. Read Matthew 28:1–10 while the class listens for the events and who participated in them. Receive reports. Lead a brief discussion regarding the possible significance of women arriving first at the tomb. Ask, *Why were the women there at the tomb? What prominence did the culture of Jesus' day place on women? What did the angels tell the women to do? What were these two women doing during Jesus' crucifixion (see Matt. 25:55)?* Give each class member a sheet of paper and a pen. Instruct the class to write a journal entry as either Mary Magdalene or the other Mary, telling about the experience with the angels and Jesus. Call on volunteers to read their entries and discuss them.

4. Invite the class to name people of authority (offices) in our culture. (Examples: police officer; mayor; governor; president of the United States; judge; coach, etc.) Ask, *What does it mean to have authority? What are some ways people receive authority?* Read Matthew 28:16–20, and call attention to verse 18. Ask, *Where did Jesus get his authority? Why do we need authority to make disciples?*

5. Before this session, prepare, or ask a class member to prepare, a monologue from one of Jesus' disciples. Include in the monologue points of identification, such as the disciple's name, where he lived, where he worked, how he met Jesus, and how Jesus changed his life. In addition to the facts, elaborate on the ways Jesus changed the disciple's life.

6. Show a video of a baptism (perhaps ask your church staff whether your church has any baptisms recorded on a DVD). An option is for you to describe your own baptism experience. Briefly describe the mode and meaning of baptism in your church. Ask, *Why did Jesus tell his followers to baptize disciples?*

7. Display a mixing bowl, a stirring spoon, an oven mitt, and a cov-
    ered cooking pan. Hide a gingerbread man cookie in the pan to use
    at the end of this section. Inform the members that today you are
    going to make a special recipe. Today, with their help, you are going
    to bake a *Delightful Disciple Dessert*. Distribute index cards, and
    lead the class in listing necessary ingredients in making a disciple.
    As people share an idea for an ingredient, tell them to write it on
    the index card and put it in the mixing bowl. Performing your best
    chef routine, mix up the ingredients, pour them in the covered pan,
    and pull out the gingerbread man cookie.

Encourage Application

8. Give people a piece of the cookie and encourage them to use it
    as a starter piece for making another disciple. Write the follow-
    ing phrase on a markerboard, "One thing I can do to help make a
    disciple is. . . ." Write answers on the board. Remind the class that
    Jesus' commission is for the entire church and that we can all play
    a part in making disciples.

Teaching Plan—Lecture and Questions

Connect with Life

1. Refer to the questions in the *Study Guide*. Review them briefly but
    without calling for answers at this point (see step 7). Point out that
    these are some of the things we want to try to answer as we study
    this passage of Scripture that climaxes our study of the Gospel of
    Matthew.

Guide Bible Study

2. Direct the class to read Matthew 28:1–10, 16–20 and underline every
    command or instruction given to someone in these passages. On
    the markerboard, write two headings, "Jesus' Disciples Then," and
    "Jesus' Disciples Now." Receive reports and write the commands

or instructions under "Jesus' Disciples Then." Lead the class in a discussion of the expectations Jesus placed on his disciples with him on the earth and his expectations of his disciples today. Write the expectations on the board under the correct heading. Compare and contrast the two lists.

3. Direct the class to Matthew 28:1–10. Point out that Mary Magdalene and another Mary were the first at the tomb after the resurrection. Give a brief description of Mary Magdalene using Matthew 28:1 for information. Ask, *Why was Mary Magdalene a follower of Jesus? After witnessing the events at the tomb, what were these women going to do? What were the women going to tell the disciples? What made their story credible? Why did Jesus want his disciples to go to Galilee?* (For guidance for answers, see the *Study Guide* and "Bible Comments" in this *Teaching Guide*.)

4. Read Matthew 28:8–10, 16–17. Ask, *How did the women and the disciples respond to Jesus? After they worshiped him, what did Jesus do in both occasions?* (Commanded to "go and tell.")

5. Ask, *According to verses 19–20, how can a person measure success in fulfilling Jesus commission?* (Did you "make disciples"?) *What is a commission?* Explain that a commission is a task given to a person with the expectation for results. In addition, the word Jesus used for "go" can be translated as *as you are going*. Ask, *What did Jesus suggest by this statement? What are some ways today that we can obey Jesus' command to go?*

6. Use these questions to guide discussion:

   (1) Why did Jesus tell his disciples that he had received all authority?

   (2) Why is authority necessary to make disciples?

   (3) How did knowing Jesus had all authority encourage his followers?

   (4) What are some synonyms for the word *disciple*?

   (5) What did Jesus mean when he told his followers to teach disciples to obey everything he commanded them?

   (6) What did Jesus command them?

(7) In addition to teaching, what did Jesus command his
disciples to do to new disciples? (baptize)

For resource information, see the *Study Guide* and "Bible
Comments" in this *Teaching Guide*.

Encourage Application

7. Return to the questions in the *Study Guide*. Ask each question, and
invite responses. Discuss ministries and programs your church
offers for making disciples. Discuss other ways the participants
can help make disciples. Use the information in "Implications and
Actions" and "How to Apply This Lesson" in the *Study Guide* to
help participants apply the Scripture passages to their lives.

FOCAL TEXT
Matthew 25:31–46

BACKGROUND
Matthew 25:31–46

MAIN IDEA
The exalted Son of Man
demonstrates concern for
the lowliest and neediest of
people and demands that
his followers do the same.

QUESTION TO EXPLORE
Helping hungry, thirsty,
poorly-clothed, sick,
imprisoned people is just
an option, isn't it?

TEACHING AIM
To help adults decide on
ways they will prepare for
the final examination

BONUS LESSON

Jesus and Hurting People

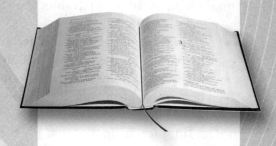

BIBLE COMMENTS

Understanding the Context

Matthew 16:21—18:35 tells of Jesus' final ministries in Galilee as he prepared his disciples for the coming conflicts with the Jewish leaders. Then Matthew 19:1—25:46 describes in a mixture of narrative and discourse the final journey to Jerusalem and the mounting conflict with the Jewish leaders. Matthew did not mention Jesus' other visits to Jerusalem (as in John's Gospel) but told only of this final, climactic journey.

These chapters underline Jesus' teaching to his disciples and his indications of his approaching sacrifice. In these discussions, Matthew recalls many of the most distinctive teachings of Jesus. Jesus discussed with his disciples the problems of divorce, taught about himself and children, and spoke of the rich man and eternal life. Jesus corrected the inappropriate seeking of first place by James and John and cleansed the temple. In Matthew 22:41–46, Jesus made a definitive statement of his messiahship.

Beginning in Matthew 23:1, Matthew recounted Jesus' teachings concerning judgment—against both Israel and the nations. In fact, chapters 23—25 can be interpreted as the fifth of the five major sections of Matthew's Gospel. Matthew emphasized teachings on the Second Coming and commanded perpetual vigilance (Matthew 24:36—25:46). He insisted that only the Father knows the exact time for Christ's return (Matt. 4:36–42). He delivered teachings concerning the necessity of perpetual vigilance in four parables:

- The parable of the householder and thief (24:43–44)
- The parable of the faithful and unfaithful servants (24:45–51)
- The parable of the ten bridesmaids (25:1–13)
- The parable of the talents (25:14–30).

The final teaching, the text for this lesson, described the judgment as a separation as between the sheep and goats (25:31–46). Jesus had initiated these discourses by focusing on the temporal judgment of Israel, but he climaxed the teaching by emphasizing the eternal judgment on the entire world.

Interpreting the Scriptures

Today's text is not a parable in the strict sense but a description of judgment. The words have a clarity and vividness seldom equaled. The lesson is that God will judge all humankind in accordance to their response to human need. God's judgment rests not on the knowledge we have gained, the fame we have acquired, the fortunes we have amassed, the powers we have assumed, or the successes we have achieved. God's judgment takes into account the help we have given to others.

That we are judged by the help we give others in no way suggests a salvation by works. Our service to those in need does not win God's grace. The clear reality is that our response to people in need demonstrates and reveals our relationship with Jesus Christ. Loving service to others grows out of our Christlikeness. Such service is the natural and inevitable reaction of redeemed people. The presence of this loving service does not earn one a right relationship with God, but the presence of service indicates that such a relationship does exist.

The Great Division (25:31–33)

25:31. Jesus described his return in glory with the angels with imagery that reflects Matthew 16:27–28 and 24:30–31. The Son of Man on his glorious throne echoes Matthew 19:28. The entire event represents a fulfillment of the vision of Daniel 7 and Zechariah 14:5. Matthew went beyond the revelation of Daniel in that now the Son of Man is on the judgment throne. John indicated that the Father had given judgment to the Son (John 5:19–29). The description of the judgment is one of grandeur, majesty, and authority.

25:32. All nations come before the King. The word translated "nations" could mean either *peoples* or *Gentiles*. In other places the term includes both Jews and Gentiles. The shift from "nations" to "peoples" (literally, *them*) suggests Jesus meant *all peoples* more than nations or even people groups. The picture is of all humanity standing before Christ in judgment.

The imagery of the sheep and goats points out and emphasizes the division between two groups that had been mixed until that time. Goats and sheep can mix together and can be difficult to separate at a superficial glance. The point is that no middle ground exists between the saved and the lost. Sheep in the Old Testament often symbolize God's people. The separation is real, frightening, and absolute.

25:33. The right hand and the left hand often contrasted favor and disfavor, accepted and unaccepted, good fortune and bad fortune. By their refusal to enter into relationship with God, those on the left hand (out of favor with God) chose their own destiny. By their willingness to enter fellowship with God in Christ, those on the right hand received the blessings God intended for them. The words recall Ezekiel 34:17–31.

The Basis for the Division (25:34–45)

25:34. The King says to those on the right hand that they should come and inherit the kingdom that is prepared for them from the creation of the world. The idea is that the blessed would enter the kingdom and share in the authority of the Christ. This kingdom and the blessing associated with it is certain, sure, and unalterable. The kingdom of God is that sphere where God reigns and blesses his people. Believers can hold absolute and solid assurance about their participation in the kingdom.

25:35–36. God had intended from the beginning of creation to create a community for fellowship with himself. The sheep are blessed because their behavior indicated their relationship with the Master that was evidenced by meeting the basic needs of people.

They fed Christ when he was hungry and gave him something to drink when he was thirsty. They cared for the stranger, that is, the foreigner who often lived in need among the people. The blessed provided clothing when the person was not adequately clad. The word does not mean *naked* as often translated but one not fully clothed as in only the undergarments. The stress is on people with less clothing than they need. These blessed persons provide companionship to those who are suffering. The words are strikingly similar to those in Isaiah 58:7.

Those who follow Jesus Christ and his way of life respond as Christ's people by meeting all the needs of people around them—the needs of salvation, nourishment, water, shelter, and companionship. Christians should realize that we can care for the physical needs of food, clothing, and even shelter but forget the necessity of companionship. Christians seek to meet every need that arises in the lives of people in this world.

25:37–39. The righteous people are surprised at Jesus' words. The term "righteous" usually denotes character or behavior but can also mean those acquitted or declared right with God. The second probably is the meaning here. The righteous are not surprised that they are in right relationship with God but that they are commended as Jesus indicated. They had not realized that in serving others they also were serving Jesus.

25:40. The King, the Son of Man, replied that these followers had cared for him when they performed acts of kindness and help to "one of the least of these brothers of mine." Several interpretations have sought to explain this last phrase.

One view considers the phrase to mean some of or all of Christ's disciples. The term "least" means *little ones*. Matthew regularly used this term to refer to Jesus' disciples (Matt. 10:42; 18:6, 10, 14). The term "brothers" in Matthew and in the New Testament is often used to identify spiritual kin.[1] Following this line of thinking, the phrase refers to all of Jesus' followers.

Another point of view sees the people described in the phrase to be primarily the followers of Jesus who need help in carrying out his mission. The "brothers" thus are itinerant missionaries, who often found themselves in need. This interpretation makes Matthew 25:39 fit well with Matthew 10:42.

Many interpreters consider the phrase to refer to any human who is in need. Significant material exists in Scripture to indicate that God desires his people to care for the poor, the widows, and those in difficult situations (see Amos, Isaiah, Luke, and James).

We gain little by pushing the interpretation of this phrase too far. It is better to accept that Jesus was indicating that service to humanity is service to him. It is better not to restrict these words to any smaller group of people. God's people are those whose works of loving care demonstrate that they have responded properly to Christ's message and become a part of his family.

25:41. The discussion is repeated for those on the left hand with some distinct differences. The people on the left hand are called "cursed."

They are ordered to depart from him, that is, suffer the loss of fellowship with the King. The "eternal fire" is prepared not for the cursed but for the devil and his angels. People who reject God's Messiah, Jesus Christ, choose to join those for whom the fire was prepared.

25:42–45. The goats ask the same types of questions as did the sheep about service to others. The Son of Man's reply indicates that the sins of omission are equally serious as those of commission. Failure to respond to Christ's message leads to eternal loss.

The Final Result of the Division (25:46)

The final verse in this passage maintains the distinction of the destinies of the two groups. Only two kinds of people exist in this world, and only two kinds will continue in the next—those who have responded positively to God's offer and those who have not.

The word "eternal" describes the state of both the good and the wicked. The passage contains no idea of annihilation of the wicked. The eternal nature of the reward of believers is exactly mirrored to the loss of the condemned. Both states are eternal. Believers should accept this fact with all its difficulties and tragedies and act lovingly to evangelize all unbelievers.

Focusing on the Meaning

The meaning of this account underlines the truth that salvation is totally by grace and in no way depends on works. Caring for the needy and downtrodden of the world does not earn salvation. Such care, an imperative for believers, flows directly from one's relationship with God.

Loving care is part of the spiritual *DNA* of Christians. Any attempt to teach and live out the pure gospel without caring for needy people is to teach and practice a mutilated gospel. Jesus indicated his concern for needy people; those who follow Jesus can do no less.

Christians should accept the heartbreaking truth that all people actually fall into one of two groups—those who acknowledge and accept Christ and those who do not. We could wish that this were not true. We greatly desire that all would be in the redeemed camp. The truth is that many will doom themselves into the group of those separated from God—the unsaved. Christians take no pleasure in the eternal punishment of the unsaved.

The state of those declared right with God through their commitment to Jesus Christ is eternal, that is, everlasting. The state of those who reject and refuse to enter a relationship with Jesus Christ is also eternal. Christians take no pleasure in the truth that the separation between the two groups is eternal.

Because of the truth of the great division, Christians should act decisively in world evangelism. The millions who have by their rebellion placed themselves in imminent danger of eternal separation must hear the Message of a forgiving God and redeeming Christ. No excuse exists for Christians neglecting the global witness. The numbers of the lost and their frightening destiny demands intensive evangelism.

The witness of believers must be in *both word and deed*. The reality of the redeemed life must be expressed in loving actions to others as well as faithfully spoken witness to the lost. Christians are not faithful to God or to their own natures as followers of God if they neglect either form of witness. We must speak the word of salvation to all people. We must express our natures as redeemed persons.

TEACHING PLANS

Teaching Plan—Varied Learning Activities

Connect with Life

1. Research (or enlist someone to research and report) the demographic information on your local area (town, city, county) to determine how many people are homeless, how many people go hungry, how many children are on free lunch programs in the schools, what the unemployment rate is, and how many people live below poverty level. Display this information on posters in different places in the room. Include the information regarding orphans

from the "Implications and Actions" section of the *Study Guide*. In addition to these posters, cut out pictures of people from magazines and add them to the posters or place them independently around the room. Call attention to the posters as you begin the lesson, and note that the lesson will deal with "Jesus and Hurting People," including these, and with what our responsibilities as Christians is regarding "hurting people."

Guide Bible Study

2. To set the context for this passage of Scripture, lead the class to review quickly Matthew 17—24 by turning through the pages of their Bibles with you and calling out the headings on the pages. Interject statements from "In the Background" in the *Study Guide* and "Understanding the Context" in this *Teaching Guide* as seems helpful.

3. Read Matthew 25:31–33 while the group listens for the main point. Ask, *What is the main point in these verses?* (the judgment) Display a picture of a goat and ask the class to share what they know about goats. Display a picture of a sheep and ask the same question about sheep. Share the information about sheep and goats under "Judgment Teaching: The Sheep and the Goats" in the *Study Guide* and under "The Great Division" in this *Teaching Guide.*

4. Point out the word "nations" in verse 32, and explain it that it refers to *all the nations*, meaning *all the people*, of the world. Explain further using information on this verse in the *Study Guide* and in "Bible Comments" in this *Teaching Guide.*

5. Enlist someone to read aloud 25:34–46 while a third of the class listens for the basis of judgment, a third listens for the responses of each group, and a third listens for the various kinds of needs mentioned. Focus on the needs. Enlist in advance someone (perhaps in your class) who is familiar with the needs of people in your community. Ask the person to tell in about five minutes about some of the human needs that exist and how individuals, classes, and your church can assist in meeting them, elaborating on some of the information on the posters. Also enlist in advance someone who

BONUS LESSON: *Jesus and Hurting People*

is familiar with how your church is seeking to meet the needs of people in your community and how people can become involved. Make three columns on the board. As each report is made, write ideas in the appropriate column—"Needs" and "What We Are Doing." After the presentations, begin to fill in the third column— "What We Need to Do."

Encourage Application

6. Refer to the three columns. Ask the class to reflect on what their willingness to help people in need says about their relationship to God. Lead the class to consider designing a ministry project, to connect to an existing ministry in your church, or to connect to another ministry in your community.

7. Purchase and distribute inexpensive plastic sunglasses. Inform the class that these special glasses will enable them to see people in need. Close in prayer and ask God to make your hearts sensitive to people in need as Jesus described in this passage.

Teaching Plans—Lecture and Questions

Connect with Life

1. Before the class, write this question on the markerboard, "How will God judge people at the Judgment?" Refer to the Question to Explore, "Helping hungry, thirsty, poorly-clothed, sick, imprisoned people is just an option, isn't it?" After a few minutes, display a poster on which you wrote, "Whatever you did for one of the least of these brothers of mine, you did for me."

Guide Bible Study

2. Read Matthew 25:31–46 while the class listens for the main point. Use information in the *Study Guide* and "Bible Comments" in this *Teaching Guide* to explain the passage. Be sure to explain "nations"

and "these brothers of mine" (Matt. 25:40, NIV). See information on 25:32 and 25:40 in "Bible Comments" in this *Teaching Guide* to explain these concepts.

3. Direct the class to Matthew 25:34–40. Point out that the criteria Jesus uses to determine the righteous from the unrighteous in this story is how each treated people in need. Ask, *What does this teach about righteousness, obedience, and salvation? What is the correlation between acts of kindness and salvation? Is Jesus saying our works save us?* For guidance on these questions, see comments in "The Way of the Sheep" in the *Study Guide* and "Focusing on the Meaning" in this *Teaching Guide*.

Encourage Application

4. Ask the class to share ways they have helped people in need. Share an experience of your own. Ask, *Why did you choose to serve people in need? How did the experience affect you?*

5. Refer to and review with the class "Implications and Actions" and "How to Apply This Lesson" in the *Study Guide*. Lead the class to consider how they can put this Scripture passage into action and so be ready for the "final examination."

6. Close in prayer that we will show our relationship to Christ by how we serve and help other people and that we will be found faithful to Christ by how we treat "the least of these."

N O T E S

1. Craig L. Blomberg, *Matthew*, The New American Commentary (Nashville: Broadman Press, 1992), 377–378.

How to Order More Bible Study Materials

It's easy! Just fill in the following information. For additional Bible study materials, see www.baptistwaypress.org or get a complete order form of available materials by calling 1-866-249-1799 or e-mailing baptistway@bgct.org.

Title of item	Price	Quantity	Cost
This Issue:			
Matthew: Hope in the Resurrected Christ—Study Guide (BWP001066)	$3.25	_____	_____
Matthew: Hope in the Resurrected Christ—Large Print Study Guide (BWP001067)	$3.55	_____	_____
Matthew: Hope in the Resurrected Christ—Teaching Guide (BWP001068)	$3.75	_____	_____
Additional Issues Available:			
Growing Together in Christ—Study Guide (BWP001036)	$3.25	_____	_____
Growing Together in Christ—Large Print Study Guide (BWP001037)	$3.55	_____	_____
Growing Together in Christ—Teaching Guide (BWP001038)	$3.75	_____	_____
Genesis 12—50: Family Matters—Study Guide (BWP000034)	$1.95	_____	_____
Genesis 12—50: Family Matters—Teaching Guide (BWP000035)	$2.45	_____	_____
Leviticus, Numbers, Deuteronomy—Study Guide (BWP000053)	$2.35	_____	_____
Leviticus, Numbers, Deuteronomy—Large Print Study Guide (BWP000052)	$2.35	_____	_____
Leviticus, Numbers, Deuteronomy—Teaching Guide (BWP000054)	$2.95	_____	_____
Joshua, Judges—Study Guide (BWP000047)	$2.35	_____	_____
Joshua, Judges—Large Print Study Guide (BWP000046)	$2.35	_____	_____
Joshua, Judges—Teaching Guide (BWP000048)	$2.95	_____	_____
1 and 2 Samuel—Study Guide (BWP000002)	$2.35	_____	_____
1 and 2 Samuel—Large Print Study Guide (BWP000001)	$2.35	_____	_____
1 and 2 Samuel—Teaching Guide (BWP000003)	$2.95	_____	_____
1 and 2 Kings: Leaders and Followers—Study Guide (BWP001025)	$2.95	_____	_____
1 and 2 Kings: Leaders and Followers Large Print Study Guide (BWP001026)	$3.15	_____	_____
1 and 2 Kings: Leaders and Followers Teaching Guide (BWP001027)	$3.45	_____	_____
Job, Ecclesiastes, Habakkuk, Lamentations: Dealing with Hard Times—Study Guide (BWP001016)	$2.75	_____	_____
Job, Ecclesiastes, Habakkuk, Lamentations: Dealing with Hard Times—Large Print Study Guide (BWP001017)	$2.85	_____	_____
Job, Ecclesiastes, Habakkuk, Lamentations: Dealing with Hard Times—Teaching Guide (BWP001018)	$3.25	_____	_____
Psalms and Proverbs: Songs and Sayings of Faith—Study Guide (BWP001000)	$2.75	_____	_____
Psalms and Proverbs: Songs and Sayings of Faith—Large Print Study Guide (BWP001001)	$2.85	_____	_____
Psalms and Proverbs: Songs and Sayings of Faith—Teaching Guide (BWP001002)	$3.25	_____	_____
Mark: Jesus' Works and Words—Study Guide (BWP001022)	$2.95	_____	_____
Mark: Jesus' Works and Words—Large Print Study Guide (BWP001023)	$3.15	_____	_____
Mark:Jesus' Works and Words—Teaching Guide (BWP001024)	$3.45	_____	_____
Jesus in the Gospel of Mark—Study Guide (BWP000066)	$1.95	_____	_____
Jesus in the Gospel of Mark—Large Print Study Guide (BWP000065)	$1.95	_____	_____
Jesus in the Gospel of Mark—Teaching Guide (BWP000067)	$2.45	_____	_____
Luke: Journeying to the Cross—Study Guide (BWP000057)	$2.35	_____	_____
Luke: Journeying to the Cross—Large Print Study Guide (BWP000056)	$2.35	_____	_____
Luke: Journeying to the Cross—Teaching Guide (BWP000058)	$2.95	_____	_____
The Gospel of John: The Word Became Flesh—Study Guide (BWP001008)	$2.75	_____	_____
The Gospel of John: The Word Became Flesh—Large Print Study Guide (BWP001009)	$2.85	_____	_____
The Gospel of John: The Word Became Flesh—Teaching Guide (BWP001010)	$3.25	_____	_____
Acts: Toward Being a Missional Church—Study Guide (BWP001013)	$2.75	_____	_____
Acts: Toward Being a Missional Church—Large Print Study Guide (BWP001014)	$2.85	_____	_____
Acts: Toward Being a Missional Church—Teaching Guide (BWP001015)	$3.25	_____	_____
Romans: What God Is Up To—Study Guide (BWP001019)	$2.95	_____	_____
Romans: What God Is Up To—Large Print Study Guide (BWP001020)	$3.15	_____	_____
Romans: What God Is Up To—Teaching Guide (BWP001021)	$3.45	_____	_____

Ephesians, Philippians, Colossians—Study Guide (BWP001060)	$3.25	_____	_____
Ephesians, Philippians, Colossians—Large Print Study Guide (BWP001061)	$3.55	_____	_____
Ephesians, Philippians, Colossians—Teaching Guide (BWP001062)	$3.75	_____	_____
1, 2 Timothy, Titus, Philemon—Study Guide (BWP000092)	$2.75	_____	_____
1, 2 Timothy, Titus, Philemon—Large Print Study Guide (BWP000091)	$2.85	_____	_____
1, 2 Timothy, Titus, Philemon—Teaching Guide (BWP000093)	$3.25	_____	_____
Revelation—Study Guide (BWP000084)	$2.35	_____	_____
Revelation—Large Print Study Guide (BWP000083)	$2.35	_____	_____
Revelation—Teaching Guide (BWP000085)	$2.95	_____	_____

Coming for use beginning December 2008

Ezra, Haggai, Zechariah, Nehemiah, Malachi—Study Guide (BWP001071)	$3.25	_____	_____
Ezra, Haggai, Zechariah, Nehemiah, Malachi—Large Print Study Guide (BWP001072)	$3.55	_____	_____
Ezra, Haggai, Zechariah, Nehemiah, Malachi—Teaching Guide (BWP001073)	$3.75	_____	_____

Standard (UPS/Mail) Shipping Charges*	
Order Value	Shipping charge**
$.01—$9.99	$6.50
$10.00—$19.99	$8.00
$20.00—$39.99	$9.00
$40.00—$59.99	$10.00
$60.00—$79.99	$11.00
$80.00—$99.99	$12.00
$100.00—$129.99	$14.00
$130.00—$159.99	$18.00
$160.00—$199.99	$22.00
$200.00—$249.99	$26.00
$250.00—$299.99	$28.00
$300.00—$349.99	$32.00
$350.00—$399.99	$40.00
$400.00—$499.99	$48.00
$500.00—$599.99	$58.00
$600.00—$799.99	$70.00**

Cost of items (Order value) _____

Shipping charges (see chart*) _____

TOTAL _____

*Plus, applicable taxes for individuals and other taxable entities (not churches) within Texas will be added. Please call 1-866-249-1799 if the exact amount is needed prior to ordering.

**For order values $800.00 and above, please call 1-866-249-1799 or check www.baptistwaypress.org

Please allow three weeks for standard delivery. For express shipping service: Call 1-866-249-1799 for information on additional charges.

YOUR NAME _____ PHONE _____

YOUR CHURCH _____ DATE ORDERED _____

MAILING ADDRESS _____

CITY _____ STATE _____ ZIP CODE _____

MAIL this form with your check for the total amount to
BAPTISTWAY PRESS, Baptist General Convention of Texas,
333 North Washington, Dallas, TX 75246-1798
(Make checks to "Baptist Executive Board.")

OR, **FAX** your order anytime to: 214-828-5376, and we will bill you.

OR, **CALL** your order toll-free: 1-866-249-1799
(M-Th 8:30 a.m.-6:00 p.m.; Fri 8:30 a.m.-5:00 p.m. central time),
and we will bill you.

OR, **E-MAIL** your order to our internet e-mail address:
baptistway@bgct.org, and we will bill you.

OR, **ORDER ONLINE** at www.baptistwaypress.org.

We look forward to receiving your order! Thank you!